WINNEBAGO COUNTY BEER

A HEADY HISTORY

LEE REIHERZER

AMERICAN PALATE

Published by American Palate
A Division of The History Press
Charleston, SC
www.historypress.com

Cover image courtesy of Kris Larson.
Images are from author's collection unless otherwise noted.

First published 2019

Manufactured in the United States

ISBN 9781467140065

Library of Congress Control Number: 2018963661

For Denise, a modern woman who loves that old, dark lager

CONTENTS

ACKNOWLEDGEMENTS

A word of thanks to a few people who went well out of their way to help make this book happen. They say beer people are good people. These are some of the best…

Ron Akin, who has had more to do with me being able to do this than he'll ever realize.

The late John Raymond Allen, who shared his family's stories about the hop-farming days in Allenville.

Leigh Aschbrenner, for helping me out when I didn't even know I needed it.

John Fritsch and Stan Sevenich, a couple of good guys from Menasha who invited a stranger into their homes and allowed me to paw through their collections of breweriana.

Doug Hoverson, who's better at this stuff than I am and always willing to help. Doug has taken on the massive project of documenting the brewing history of all of Wisconsin. Look for Doug's books!

Kay Kuenzl-Stenerson, for sharing her family's history in the beer business and helping me get at stories behind the story.

Alan Lareau, whose skill at translating old German text has saved me from extreme embarrassment.

Dan Radig, who has been incredibly generous to me and so many others, sharing his knowledge of our local history and his unparalleled collection of images.

Steve Schrage, whose passion for preserving rare beer bottles opened up the world of those old, independent bottlers to me.

ACKNOWLEDGEMENTS

John Steiner, whom I hadn't even met before I came asking for help. He immediately came to my aid.

Wayne and Suzanne Youngwirth, who gave freely of their time so I could have a more complete picture of Wayne's bootlegging grandfather. Oh, the stories!

Brian Zenefski, for connecting me to people I needed to know to get the story straight.

Everybody at the Winnefox Library System. The libraries in this county are incredible and staffed with some of the sharpest, most helpful people you will ever meet.

All of our local brewers, who have been endlessly patient with my endless questioning over the years.

The best for last…without Denise Lanthier, this book would not have been even remotely possible.

INTRODUCTION

If you were to select a single Wisconsin county most representative of the state's celebrated history of beer making, you could do no better than look to Winnebago County. Though Milwaukee's contribution to brewing is better known, its large, industrial breweries were outliers. A more accurate picture of Wisconsin brewing is drawn from the hundreds of small breweries that established the state's beer culture. Winnebago County is a microcosm of that tradition. The story of beer in this place on the western shore of Lake Winnebago is uniquely emblematic of the history of beer in Wisconsin both past and present.

Over the last 170 years, Winnebago County has been home to thirty-one breweries. The first of those was launched in 1849 following the arrival of a young German immigrant to Oshkosh. From there it spread, first to Menasha and then to Butte des Morts, Neenah and Winneconne. These brewers shared more than just common ground. Their histories intermingle.

The breweries ranged in size. In the beginning, they operated as small, community-based businesses producing just a few hundred barrels of beer annually. The European influence of their founders was pronounced, but that wore away as the years wore on. The beer changed, too. It took on an American character, and the breweries grew larger. Those that couldn't adapt failed. The survivors became regional concerns, sending their beer across the state. In the end, even they couldn't compete in an industry transformed by consolidation.

INTRODUCTION

For almost twenty years, beginning in the 1970s, Winnebago County was without a brewery. It had never been this way before, not even during Prohibition, when brewing was outlawed. Despite the loss, the county's beer culture endured. It was kept alive by hobbyists and preservationists. It was revived nightly in neighborhood taverns that could trace their histories back a century or more. Some of those places still bore the marks of the breweries that built them. It was not the end of the story, it was an intermission—the completion of the first cycle.

In 1991, brewing returned. The approach of those who spearheaded the revival was surprisingly similar to that of the first brewers who arrived in the mid-1800s. It began, again, in Oshkosh, and again, from there it spread. The resurgence is still underway.

This is a raucous story full of pioneers, adventurers, swindlers and entrepreneurs—people who pushed their luck to its absolute limit. Some risked almost everything to create a tradition of their own. And around them developed a culture with a flavor all its own. Against all odds, this lineage continues to inform the present. This is the story of Winnebago County beer.

A CHRONOLOGY OF WINNEBAGO COUNTY BREWERIES

1. THE LAKE BREWERY, 1849–68
Oshkosh, east side of Lake Street, approximately one hundred yards south of Ceape Avenue
   1849–53: Jacob Konrad
   1853–62: Anton Andrea
   1862–65: Leonhardt Schwalm
   1865–68: Gottlieb Ecke

2. JOSEPH SCHUSSLER'S OSHKOSH BREWERY, 1849–52
Oshkosh, south side of Bay Shore Drive, midway between Bowen and Frankfort Streets

3. SPERRY, O'CONNELL, HALL AND LOESCHER, 1850–56
Menasha, south side of River Street, approximately two hundred yards west of Washington Street
   1850–51: Alanson Sperry and Edward O'Connell
   1851–53: Alanson Sperry and Orville Hall
   1853–56: Orville Hall and Frederick Loescher

4. LOESCHER'S (FIRST) OSHKOSH BREWERY, 1852–78
Oshkosh, 1253–83 Bay Shore Drive
   1852–53: George and Frederick Loescher
   1853–78: George Loescher

5. Hall and Loescher, Merz and Behre, Winz, Menasha Brewing Company, 1856–1920
Menasha, northeast corner of Manitowoc and First Streets (Winz Park)
    1856–71: Orville Hall and Frederick Loescher
    1871–80: Herman Merz and George Behre
    1880: Werner Winz
    1881–89: Werner Winz and Frederick Loescher
    1889–1920: Menasha Brewing Company

6. Neenah Brewery, 1856–1911
Neenah, approximately 129 North Lake Street
    1856–72: Jacob Lachmann
    1872–74: Frank Ehrgott
    1874–82: Adam and Frank Ehrgott
    1882–1901: Adam Ehrgott
    1901–5: Henry Angermeyer
    1906–10: Oscar Doerr
    1910–11: Louis Sorenson

7. Fischer, Weist and Kaehler, 1856–1858
Oshkosh, near the southwest corner of High and New York Avenues
    1856–57: Tobias Fischer and August Weist
    1857–58: Tobias Fischer and Christian Kaehler

8. Joseph Dudler's Brewery, approximately 1856–57
Menasha, may have been near the northeast corner of Broad and Racine Streets

9. Butte des Morts Brewery, 1857–80?
Butte des Morts, south side of Washington Street between Ontario and Main Streets
    1857–62: Christoph Klenk
    1862–65: Louis Schwalm
    1865: Leonhardt Schwalm
    1865–perhaps as late as 1880: Frederick Bogk

10. Busch Brewery/Fifth Ward Brewery, 1858–1880
Oshkosh, near the southeast corner of Algoma Boulevard and Vine Avenue
    1858: Tobias Fischer and Christian Kaehler, Busch Brewery
    1858–80: Christian Kaehler's Fifth Ward Brewery

11. Rudolph Otten Brewery, 1865
Oshkosh, Oxford Avenue

12. RAHR BREWING COMPANY, 1865–1956
Oshkosh, north side of Rahr Avenue near the Lake Winnebago shoreline
    1865–83: Charles and August Rahr
    1883–97: Charles Rahr's City Brewery
    1897–1917: Charles Rahr Jr./Rahr Brewing Company
    1917–56: Rahr Brewing Company of Oshkosh

13. THE ISLAND BREWERY/WALTER BROTHERS BREWING, 1866–1956
Menasha, approximately 324 Nicolet Boulevard
    1866–68: Peter and Simon Caspary and Jacob Tuchscherer
    1868–70: Joseph and Jacob Fridolin Mayer and Stephen Steubel
    1870–74: Joseph and Jacob Fridolin Mayer
    1874–79: Joseph Mayer
    1879–86: George Habermehl (with R. Mueller until 1883)
    1886–88: Edward Fueger
    1888–89: Christian and Martin Walter and Frank Fries
    1889–94: Christian and Martin Walter
    1894–1956: Walter Brothers Brewing Company

14. HORN AND SCHWALM'S BROOKLYN BREWERY, 1866–94
Oshkosh, 1630–70 Doty Street

15. THEODORE YAGER'S WINNECONNE BREWERY, 1866–84
Winneconne, east bank of the Wolf River near the end of South First Avenue

16. FRANZ WAHLE/GLATZ UNION BREWERY, 1867–94
Oshkosh, end of Doty Street (Glatz Park)
    1867–69: Franz Wahle
    1869–79: John Glatz and Christian Elser Union Brewery
    1879–88: John Glatz Union Brewery
    1888–94 John Glatz and Son (William Glatz)

17. THE GAMBRINUS BREWERY, 1868–94
Oshkosh, 1239–47 Harney Avenue
    1868–71: Gottlieb Ecke
    1871–75: Charlotte Ecke
    1875–94: Lorenz Kuenzl's Gambrinus Brewery

18. LEONARD SCHIFFMANN'S WHITE BEER BREWERY, 1870S
Oshkosh, approximately 1864 Doty Street

19. Leonard Arnold Brewery, approximately 1875–78
Oshkosh, southeast corner of Sixteenth Avenue and South Main Street

20. Frederick Voelkel Brewery, late 1870s.
Oshkosh, Northwest corner of Doty Street and West Seventeenth Avenue

21. Loescher's (Second) Oshkosh Brewery, 1880–89
Oshkosh, Northeast corner of Frankfort Street and Bay Shore Drive
    1880–84: George Loescher
    1884–89: William Loescher

22. Oshkosh Brewing Company, 1894–1971
Oshkosh, 1642 Doty Street

23. Peoples Brewing Company, 1913–72
Oshkosh, 1512 South Main Street

24. Fox Valley Brewing Company, 1940–42
Menasha, 105 Manitowoc Street

25. Mid-Coast Brewing Company, 1991–95
Oshkosh, 35 Wisconsin Street (beer produced in Stevens Point)

26. Fox River Brewing Company, established 1995
Oshkosh, 1501 Arboretum Drive

27. Bare Bones Brewery, established 2015
Oshkosh, 4362 County Highway S

28. Lion's Tail Brewing Company, established 2015
Neenah, 116 South Commercial Street

29. Fifth Ward Brewing Company, established 2017
Oshkosh, 1009 South Main Street

30. Omega Brewing Experience, established 2017
Omro, 115 East Main Street

31. HighHolder Brewing Company, established 2018
Oshkosh, 2211 Oregon Street

1

AND THEN CAME BEER

I t was an idyllic land that had gone essentially unchanged for centuries. It was where a prairie gave way to an expansive forest covering what would become northern Wisconsin. This was transitional space. The gently sloping landscape was blanketed by wildflowers and tall grasses. The grasslands were relieved by groves of bur oak. Further north, the oak stands gave way to pinery.

Native tribes had populated those lands longer than memory could recall. They were seminomadic. Their survival depended on hunting, gathering and simple agriculture. Among them were the Potawatomi, the Sauk and the Fox. The Menominee and the Winnebago had been there the longest. They were there when the change came. And when it came, it was brutal.

The first Europeans traveled through the area in 1634. They were missionaries. The initial encounters were peaceful enough. But tensions rose as the Europeans turned from harvesting souls to harvesting resources. The native tribes found themselves in competition with European fur traders working the waterways. Clashes were inevitable. In 1716, it turned to all-out war. The Europeans kept coming. After the War of 1812, Americans began to arrive. By the end of the 1820s, the native tribes were overwhelmed.

In a set of treaties, the last signed in 1836, the Menominee Indian Nation ceded more than six million acres of its land to the United States. What would become Winnebago County was part of that territory. The 1836 treaty had been signed by the tribe's Chief Oshkosh. His name would be attached to a city and coopted by breweries operating there in years to come. By then, it was a whole other place.

The transformation began gradually. Permanent settlers were putting down roots even before the Menomonee had relinquished their land. The newcomers brought their own customs, including a predilection for drink. The first approximation of a tavern went up near the site of the present-day village of Butte des Morts. It was launched in 1818 by traders Augustin Grignon and Jaques Porlier. Though their establishment was a trading post, Grignon and Porlier also served liquor. Wisconsin pioneer Albert G. Ellis wrote that Grignon was known for "his princely hospitality. His

An illustration of Chief Oshkosh from an 1855 daguerreotype.

house was often crowded at night to the great inconvenience of himself and family." Patrons of the outpost were said to include future U.S. president Zachary Taylor and the future president of the Confederacy, Jefferson Davis. Grignon's log cabin was the forerunner to the colorful saloon culture that would come to flourish in Butte des Morts.

The first Winnebago County tavern that would identify as such was established in Oshkosh about 1832. Its proprietor was George Johnston. He arrived in the area after serving in the War of 1812. Johnston set up shop on the south end of what is now Riverside Cemetery off Algoma Boulevard. From there, he ran his tavern and a ferry service carrying travelers over the Fox River. But Johnston couldn't make a go of it. In 1835, he sold out to James Knaggs, who operated in much the same manner as his predecessor. Knaggs also had little success with what early Winnebago County historian Publius V. Lawson described as a "wreck of a shanty." Nonetheless, the old tavern endured. In the summer of 1836, it was purchased by a Connecticut-born Yankee settler named Webster Stanley. He hauled his new old tavern downriver and replanted it on the northern shore of the Fox where it connects with Lake Winnebago.

For close to two centuries, nonnatives had been flowing through the area, but now, the new people were coming to stay. At first, they arrived in ones and twos. They were Yankees from the crowded East staking out the newly opened lands in the Northwest. It wasn't long before entire families were arriving. Stanley's Tavern was the epicenter of their community. It was where they worked out their initial attempts at governing. It served as their post office, and it was there, after a whiskey-drenched vote, they selected the name Oshkosh for the village that would become the county seat.

The census of 1840 enumerated 140 nonnative residents in what was to become Winnebago County. In the coming decade, that number would increase by more than 10,000. They settled in Neenah, Menasha and Omro. They plowed the hunting grounds to establish farms in townships that took their names from the people who had been there before—Poygan, Waukau, Nekimi, Nepeuskun and Winneconne. They drained swamps and reshaped waterways. They built dams at Neenah. They cut channels at Menasha. It was thirsty work. The beer began flowing in.

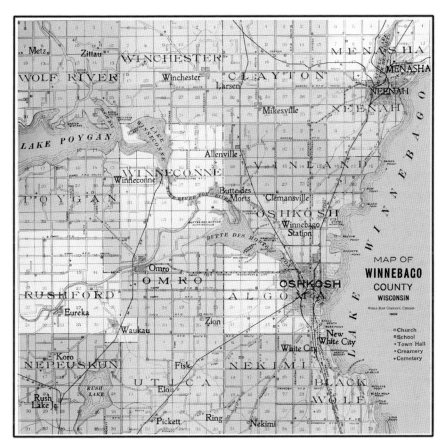

Winnebago County, 1909.

Winnebago County was officially organized in 1848. Its first newspaper was published on February 9, 1849. James Densmore, editor of the *Oshkosh True Democrat*, was a temperance advocate. He rarely missed an opportunity to rail against demon rum. The *True Democrat* was the county's paper of record and Densmore's soapbox. He featured reports on the area's growth alongside tales of the drunken debauchery that accompanied it. Densmore cheered on the development while complaining that liquor sales were increasing entirely too rapidly. But Densmore was a practical man. He knew what it took to make a buck in a place like this. The *True Democrat* was awash in advertising for saloons, liquor and beer. Those advertisements are a window onto the beer-drinking habits of early Winnebago County residents.

The majority of them had come from the East and were of English descent. They favored the English-style ales their forebears had brought with them to America. The beer advertised in the *True Democrat* reflected their preferences. Porter topped the list. At the close of the 1840s, London-brewed porters were readily available in Winnebago County. The dark, tart and bitter beer was sold by the keg and by the gallon in grocery stores and by the tankard in taverns. Michigan-brewed Detroit ale was another popular tipple. Scotch ales, Burton ales and India pale ales all had their day in the county's formative years. But for many of the new arrivals, these were beers associated with the past. These were forward-looking people. They hadn't set out for the middle of nowhere to recreate the life they had been living in the places they left. When the new thing came along, the old ales were forsaken.

That new thing was lager beer. The cool-fermented lagers were unlike the warm-fermented ales that had been predominant. Lager was typically lighter in body, lower in alcohol, less bitter and lacked the tart twang that accompanied so many ales. Though lager brewing had its roots in fifteenth-century Bavaria, it was still considered modern beer. Lager hadn't made a splash in America until about 1840. By the close of the decade, the first drafts of it were arriving in Winnebago County. It was sent in by wagons traveling from Milwaukee. People loved it. Lager beer wasn't the only German influence coming to be felt in Winnebago County. In the late 1840s, a surge of German migration was making its way into Wisconsin. Winnebago County became a destination for thousands of the newcomers. Among them were trained brewers. The time had come to produce a local beer.

2

1849-1859

THE FIRST WAVE

Friday, August 2, 1850…Jacob Konrad woke to a warm morning. It may have taken him a moment to realize where he was. Konrad was more than four thousand miles from home. Despite the distance, much of what surrounded him was remarkably familiar. He was in a brewery. Konrad wasn't yet thirty years old, and already most of his life had been spent in breweries. Through the window, he could see Lake Winnebago and the lush greenery of Oshkosh in summer. It looked a lot like where he had come from. Konrad dressed and went about his work. Later in the day, a census taker came by and asked him what he did for a living. Konrad replied, probably in German, that he ran a brewery. What was going on here? A German around the corner had said the same thing moments earlier. The first wave was underway.

Jacob Konrad was born in 1823 in Koblenz, an ancient city in western Germany where the Rhine and Moselle Rivers meet. In Koblenz, there was a long tradition of beer making. Konrad was a part of that by the time he turned fifteen and began his apprenticeship. He arrived in America in 1847 with little money. But Konrad had a skill that would make him welcome most any place he went. He went to Milwaukee, where he worked for a couple of years as a brewer. In 1849, Konrad headed for Oshkosh with enough money for a down payment on some land. He chose a spot on the shore of Lake Winnebago a short walk from where it connects with the Fox River.

On July 25, 1849, Konrad entered into an agreement to purchase two and a half acres on the east side of Lake Street. The raising of Winnebago

County's first brewery was underway. Konrad's Lake Brewery would provide the template for the brewers who followed. A brewer born and trained in Germany leaves his homeland for America and finds his way to Wisconsin. He spends a year or two working in Milwaukee breweries then heads north having earned enough money to go into business for himself. He starts by purchasing land near water. There would be few exceptions to the pattern.

It was no coincidence that it worked this way time and again. European social unrest was the lead domino. Germany was in turmoil economically and politically. The upheaval limited opportunities for brewers who had dedicated years to learning their craft. At the same time, they were hearing of a world of opportunity waiting in America. Sometimes the message was delivered in letters sent home by those who were already there. Other times, it was delivered more systematically by states like Wisconsin, which actively recruited Germans.

Many of the young brewers landed in what came to be known as the German Triangle, composed of Cincinnati, Milwaukee and St. Louis. These were already centers of brewing and destination points for those who lacked the capital to launch breweries of their own. It didn't take much to make that happen. Land in newly settled places like Winnebago County was cheap. Much of that land was waterfront property. This was a critical element for brewers intent on making the increasingly popular lager beer.

Traditional lager brewing requires a cold, slow fermentation at about 50° Fahrenheit. It's followed by an even longer period of cool maturation. Brewers would often "lager" or store their beer for months at these low temperatures—not an easy task in an era before mechanical refrigeration, but there was a way. The first step was to construct an aging cellar of stone, either underground or burrowed into the side of a hill. The next was to pack it with ice—thus the benefit of waterfront property. At the height of winter, brewers would harvest lake or river ice by the ton. Packed in sawdust, the ice would keep their cellars cool well into summer. The best cellars could maintain their chill throughout the year.

Konrad's lack of advertising was also typical of brewers in this period. He had little need for self-promotion. The people nearby knew what he was up to, and that was all that mattered. Early Winnebago County brewers didn't widely distribute their beer. Their product was sold to people living in the immediate vicinity, often from a taproom connected to the brewery. Today, we'd call them craft brewers. In the mid-1800s, these small-scale operations dominated Wisconsin's brewing landscape.

Better Than Is Obtained from Abroad

The 1850 census taker who visited Jacob Konrad had just come from another brewery. The brewer there was Joseph Schussler. On November 11, 1849, Schussler initiated the second brewery in Winnebago County when he purchased land on the shore of the Fox River where it flows into Lake Winnebago. Schussler's acre was down the block from where Webster Stanley's old tavern had been and around the corner from Konrad's Lake Brewery. The two brewers had much more in common than location. Schussler was born in the Baden territory of Germany in 1819 and at fifteen began his apprenticeship as a brewer. In 1840, he sailed to America, and he was in Milwaukee by 1846. There, he met a fellow German émigré named Johann Braun. Naturally, they launched a brewery. But Schussler couldn't stay settled. He sold out to Braun and moved on. The brewery Schussler left would eventually become Blatz Brewing. He found work at another Milwaukee brewery, this one owned by Franz Neukirch. Schussler promptly married Neukirch's daughter, Fannie, and in 1849, the couple moved to Oshkosh. The Neukirch Brewery later became part of the Pabst Brewing empire. Schussler was always a little ahead of the curve.

After establishing himself in Oshkosh, Schussler took on a business partner named John Freund. They named their enterprise the Oshkosh Brewery. They were never shy about promoting their product. The Oshkosh Brewery became the first in Winnebago County to advertise its beer. The ads always ended on the same confident note: "A superior article—better than is obtained from abroad under the title of Detroit Ale, Milwaukee Beer, & etc."

Some forty years later, Schussler was still talking about that early beer and still sounding like his old ads. He told a newspaper reporter that it was "a healthy drink. It was pure barley and hops and not corn and other adulterations as are used today." Schussler claimed his brewing method was different from others and known only to himself. Whatever he was doing was working. People quickly developed a taste for the locally produced lagers. It would remain so for more than a century. This was a local beer in the truest sense. The barley it was made with was grown nearby and malted at the brewery. Schussler and Freund regularly placed notices in the *Oshkosh True Democrat* imploring the county's farmers to bring them their harvest. They had an appealing pitch. "We will pay the highest market price in CASH, for any quantity of Barley delivered at the Oshkosh Brewery."

Schussler needed all he could get—his recipe was ingredient intensive. Schussler said he required three bushels of malted barley (144 pounds) and

BARLEY! BARLEY!!

WE will pay the highest market price in *CASH*, for any quantity of Barley delivered at the Oshkosh Brewery.
27   SCHEUSSLER & FREUND.

Oshkosh Brewery.

THE SUBSCRIBERS having erected a *BREWERY* in the village of Oshkosh, are prepared to supply the Tavern, Grocery, and Saloon keepers of the surrounding country, with good Ale and Beer. From a long experience in the business, they feel confident in warranting a superior article—better than is obtained from abroad under the title of "Detroit Ale," "Milwaukee Beer," &c.
27   SCHEUSSLER & FREUND.

An 1898 illustration of Joseph Schussler. The 1850 advertisement for Schussler's Oshkosh Brewery appeared frequently in the *Oshkosh True Democrat*.

a pound of hops to produce a single barrel of beer. He may also have been sourcing some of those hops locally. In the early 1850s, commercial hop growing in Winnebago County was getting underway. In all, it would have made for a beer fresher and more vibrant than anything that had journeyed from London, Detroit or Milwaukee. A strong demand for local beer was being established. A host of breweries rose up to meet it.

A YANKEE BREWERY

James Duane Doty wished to see a brewery in Menasha. Doty had been governor of the territory of Wisconsin from 1841 until 1844. Now he was serving Winnebago County in the U.S. House of Representatives. He also owned much of the land comprising the present city of Menasha. The congressman wanted it developed. What better augur for a growing community than its own brewery? On February 28, 1850, Doty made a deal to make it happen.

Acting through his attorney, Curtis Reed, Doty proffered several lots off River Street on the north bank of the Fox River. In addition to the land, Doty was offering to float a $2,000 line of credit (worth about $64,000 today). The contingency was that the grantees were to "forthwith commence the erection of a frame building on said lots suitable for a brewery and proceed

A ca. 1850 daguerreotype of James Duane Doty. *Courtesy of the Beinecke Rare Book & Manuscript Library, Yale University.*

as fast as practical in the erection of same to completion and commence the business of brewing there within six months." Doty was in a hurry. Surely, he was aware of what was occurring with those new breweries in Oshkosh. The men who took Doty up on his offer were Alanson K. Sperry and Edward F. O'Connell. Unlike most Winnebago County brewers of the pre–Civil War period, O'Connell and Sperry had not migrated from Germany. Sperry was thirty-five and from New York. O'Connell was twenty-four and born in Ireland. Both had arrived in Menasha within the year. Neither had much, if any, brewing experience.

O'Connell and Sperry made the tight deadline imposed by Doty. By July 1850, the brewery was up and running. It was a crowded place. Sperry lived there with his wife and their two-year-old boy. The brewery was also the home of nine other men, all of them recent arrivals from Ireland. Did that deep Irish influence extend to the beer? It's hard to imagine it didn't, but we can't know for sure. Most of the particulars concerning this early brewery have been lost to time. Whatever O'Connell and Sperry were brewing, people apparently liked it. By April 1851, Sperry had raised enough money to purchase the property outright from Doty. That spring, the *Oshkosh True Democrat* reported that Menasha "teams with improvement," with the brewery there "doing a driving business." The success was accompanied by turbulence. The union of O'Connell and Sperry had frayed. By the summer of 1851, O'Connell was out.

Sperry took on a fellow Yankee as his new partner; a man new to Menasha and new to the business of brewing. His name was Orville J. Hall. Hall was born in Vermont in 1818 but was raised on his father's farm in New York, where he received an education at one of the state's early common schools. At seventeen, he set out on his own. It's not altogether surprising that Hall wound up a brewer. He liked to try different things. Among other jobs, he had done stints as a stagecoach driver, a photographer, a shopkeeper and a dam builder. Hall liked to roam. During the 1840s, he lived in six states and Canada. By the end of the decade, he'd had his fill of that kind of life. In September 1849, the thirty-one-year-old Hall married. A few months later, he and his wife, Delilah, moved to Menasha.

Hall opened a grocery store. There were about one thousand people then living in Menasha. New businesses were going up in every direction. The dearth of saloons in such a place was uncommon. The lone Menasha saloon advertised itself as a temperance enterprise offering nothing stronger than soda water. The bulk of the liquor trade was taking place at groceries licensed to sell alcohol—places like Hall's store. It wouldn't be long before saloons began moving in. They'd need someone to supply their beer. Hall recognized opportunity there. On July 7, 1851, Hall bought a half interest in A.K. Sperry's brewery. Hall's plans for the brewery were ambitious. To realize them, he'd need the help of a German brewer who was making his way to Oshkosh.

Busted in Oshkosh

Joseph Schussler was struggling. Working with others was always something of a problem for him. He'd had his issues with his partners in Milwaukee. Now it was happening in Oshkosh.

At the start of 1851, Schussler dissolved his partnership with John Freund. Schussler immediately teamed with Francis Tillmans. It looked like a good fit. Tillmans was deeply connected within Oshkosh's growing community of beer-drinking German émigrés. Schussler remained confident as ever. He placed a notice in the *Oshkosh True Democrat* announcing the change. "We hope, by prompt attention, to continue to receive the good name the establishment has heretofore enjoyed; and we warrant our work to be unsurpassed in quality by any in the country."

Quality wasn't going to be enough. Three months after forming the partnership with Tillmans, Schussler dissolved it. Needing capital, he took out a series of loans against the brewery. Schussler soon found himself unable to keep up with the payments. The swaggering newspaper ads stopped. By the summer of 1852, he had hit bottom. That June, Schussler signed his assets over to his creditors. The Oshkosh Brewery was dismantled.

Schussler stayed in Oshkosh for the remainder of the 1850s. He made his living as a cooper and sometimes worked in other people's breweries. In the early 1860s, he moved to Fond du Lac, where he opened the West Hill Brewery. This time it worked out for him. Schussler remained a successful brewer until his retirement at the age of seventy-one.

Bavarians at the Gate

At the start of summer 1852, two breweries remained in Winnebago County: Sperry and Hall's in Menasha and Jacob Konrad's in Oshkosh. Konrad wasn't given much of a chance to enjoy his time as Oshkosh's sole brewer. In July, two Bavarian-born brothers arrived. Both were brewers. George Loescher was born in 1819. Brother Frederick came two years later. The duo set out for America in 1851. They found their way to Milwaukee and, after a short stay, left for Oshkosh. They were said to have made the eighty-five-mile journey on foot.

On September 25, 1852, the Loescher brothers bought a parcel of land off Bayshore Drive at the outlet of the Fox River into Lake Winnebago.

They immediately began building a brewery. The Loeschers didn't strain themselves coming up with a flashy title for the place. They simply reintroduced the "Oshkosh Brewery" name recently abandoned by Schussler. Which raises the question, was there an arrangement of some sort between Schussler and the Loescher brothers? If there was, it remained private. None of the recorded transactions involving the new Oshkosh Brewery include any reference to Schussler.

Their brewery comprised three buildings set back about one hundred feet from the shore of Lake Winnebago. The facilities included a malt house, the brew house and the ice-cooled cellars where the beer fermented in wooden barrels. The Loeschers' standard lager would have been dark in color, a rich brown with ruby highlights. It was an all-malt beer with enough hop-derived bitterness to balance its substantial malt profile. Their beer was intended as a sustaining beverage with an abundance of residual sugars and a mild boost of alcohol—less than 5 percent by volume. In the latter half of the 1800s, this rustic style of lager became synonymous with beer in Winnebago County. Frederick and George Loescher were instrumental in making that happen. At the close of 1853, the Loeschers' Oshkosh Brewery was a year old and growing. It was time for the younger of the brothers to set out on his own. In December, Frederick sold his share in the Oshkosh Brewery to George. Frederick already had something else in the works. He was on the move again, but this time he didn't have to travel by foot. There was now daily steamboat service running between Oshkosh and Menasha. Frederick Loescher headed north.

A DYNAMIC DUO

In the summer of 1853, the brewery on the river in Menasha celebrated its third anniversary. A.K. Sperry and Orville Hall had become experienced brewers. For Sperry, it was all the experience he cared to have. On August 10, 1853, Sperry sold his stake in the brewery to Hall, who already had a new partner in the wings. This one was a ringer from Bavaria by way of Oshkosh. Frederick Loescher had spent the previous week getting to know Menasha. Now he was going to be its new brewer in partnership with Hall. Sperry financed the arrangement. Hall looked on as Loescher signed the papers.

The new partners were an odd couple, Hall with his Yankee ways and Loescher still every bit the *Münchner*. Perhaps it was their differences that made them work so well in tandem. Among the early Winnebago County brewers, Hall and Loescher were singular. They managed to grow their brewery without burying it in debt. Their fiscal discipline was a rare skill among the brewers entering the county.

Within a couple of years, the Hall and Loescher brewery was running full out. A newspaper report from 1855 described the brewery as "extensive" and the beer coming out of it to be "of the first quality." Increasingly, that beer was finding its way out of Menasha. Hall and Loescher may have been the first brewers in Winnebago County to distribute beyond their home base. They exploited the convenience of their location on the Fox River to ship beer up to Appleton, which didn't yet have a brewery. The *Appleton Crescent* would have preferred it if Hall and Loescher had kept their beer to themselves. An 1854 editorial in the *Crescent* complained about the "nuisance" of Menasha beer and the "sundry places where Menasha beer is bought and drank" in Appleton.

The brewery's site may have been convenient, but the narrow islet it inhabited between the river and canal left little room for growth. Hall and Loescher began prospecting for a new location. They found a suitable spot about a mile away. On March 13, 1856, the duo bought a set of lots at the northeast corner of Manitowoc and First Streets. Here, they'd have all the room they needed. They weren't alone in recognizing Menasha as a growth market. While Hall and Loescher planned their move, someone else was planning to move in on their territory.

The Elusive Dudler

An 1850s brewery can be difficult to get a handle on. Many of them did not advertise. Newspapers tended to ignore them, save for fire or some hideous accident. Federal taxation of brewers was nonexistent, and local regulation was lax in the extreme. The result is that many brewers left almost no paper trail or little else to be remembered by. Some were obscure even in their own time. J. Dudler is an example of how slippery these early brewers could be. He goes entirely missing from most conventional histories of Menasha. He does, however, turn up in several chronologies of Wisconsin breweries, where Dudler is never more than a single-line entry: "J. Dudler, 1850s." Heretofore, that's been the extent of his story. There's more to tell.

His name was Joseph L. Dudler, and he was born in Switzerland about 1824. By 1848, he was in Dodge County, Wisconsin, where he married a German immigrant named Susan Knester. In April 1850, Dudler and his wife arrived in Menasha. Susan was pregnant. In September, she gave birth to their first child, a boy named Charles.

Joseph Dudler was a carpenter by trade and followed that line of work after reaching Menasha. But he kept brushing up against brewers. He lived next door to O'Connell and Sperry while they were getting their brewery up and running. And Dudler was an associate of Jacob Tuchscherer, who was also about to launch a brewery in Menasha. Somewhere along the line, Dudler developed the bug to brew. The best evidence suggests he didn't act on that impulse until about 1856.

Business listings published prior to 1856 concur that Menasha was home to a single brewery. The first indications of a second come from two works published in 1857. The first, a promotional booklet entitled *The Village of Menasha: Its Location, History, and Advantages*, enumerates two breweries but doesn't identify them by name. The second source, the *Wisconsin State Directory* of 1857–58, is more forthcoming. It attaches names to the two breweries, Hall & Loescher and J. Dudler. Neither source lists addresses. So where was Dudler's brewery? He left a hint.

In 1852, Dudler acquired a property near the northeast corner of Broad and Racine Streets. He began building it up, taking out a series of loans to finance the project. On September 9, 1856, a new detail emerges. A venue named Dudler's Hall is mentioned in the *Conservator* newspaper. At this point, Joseph Dudler is the only adult male with that name living in Menasha, and the property on Broad Street is the only one he owns in the village. Is this conclusive evidence that Dudler operated a brewery at this site? Hardly. It's a best guess. Whatever Dudler was up to, he was certainly showing the common tics of a brewer of his era.

Dudler was borrowing money with abandon. In five years, he mortgaged the property eight times. By the close of 1856, those notes were coming due. Then came the crash of 1857. Winnebago County plunged into depression. Menasha was particularly hard hit. Dudler had nowhere to turn. He pulled a typical shuffle: Dudler transferred the title of the property to a third party and then had it put in his wife's name. His shell game failed, and by 1860, the property was in foreclosure. Dudler left Menasha and took his family west. One account has them driving an ox team across the plains to Salt Lake Valley in Utah. Back in Menasha, people were still trying to sue him.

The Dudlers settled just outside of Salt Lake City in an area known as Parley's Hallow. There, Dudler established a saloon and brewery that became locally famous. The site is now part of a nature preserve with a marker honoring Dudler's accomplishments. Dudler's presence as a brewer in Menasha, however, remains more shadow than substance.

Vagabond Brewers

They left Germany expecting never to return. They parted from friends and family with goodbyes that were assumed to be forever. They boarded crowded ships and drifted away. Most had only a vague notion of where they might end up. It was terrifying and liberating. For some, the leaving unleashed a wanderlust that would continue pushing them. Jacob Konrad couldn't shake it. The urge to move was on him again. He had launched the Lake Brewery in Oshkosh five years earlier. That was time enough in one place. Konrad sold out and moved away.

The buyer was Anton Andrea, a man every bit as restless as Konrad. Andrea was born into a wealthy family in Frankfurt in 1823. His formal schooling was in Switzerland, but he got a worldlier education after joining the Hungarian Hussars in the early 1840s. By 1848, he had attained the rank of major and was on the run. With revolution sweeping across Europe, Hungary rose up to break free from the Austrian Empire. Andrea found himself facing the prospect of having to battle his own countrymen. He defected and fled to Istanbul where he slipped onto a ship bound for America. Andrea was twenty-seven when he arrived in Oshkosh in 1849.

Andrea went into overdrive. He launched, built up and bankrupted one business after another. He could sell almost anything until he lost interest. Over the years, Andrea dealt in clothes, groceries, liquor and real estate. He'd make a pile of money and then lose it all. Then he'd do it again. He spoke five languages and was followed by fire—Andrea was burned out six times. Everybody in Oshkosh knew him. They called him Major Andrea and elected him to the first Oshkosh City Council in 1853. He quit that a few months later. On October 24, 1854, the major bought a brewery. Andrea had little if any background in beer making, but lack of experience never stopped him before. He enlisted the help of two German-born brewers who took up residence in the brewery. When asked to state his own profession, Andrea would identify as a brewer, but his role within the brewery was

A bird's-eye view of Oshkosh in the mid-1850s.

limited. The beer made there was the increasingly popular dark lager. The attention it received was not always beneficial—Andrea's brewery became a target.

In late June 1859, the Lake Brewery was brimming with finished beer ready for the summer surge in demand. Saboteurs broke into Andrea's cellars and split open casks of finished beer, draining their contents over the dirt floor. Kegs ready for delivery were dosed with salt, destroying the beer inside. It was the worst possible time for something like this to happen. Andrea's stock was lost and months of work ruined. He estimated the loss at $1,000 (about $30,000 in today's money). The perpetrators were never caught.

NEENAH'S SLICE OF HELL

About 1850, a mysterious Welshman arrived in Neenah. He was known only as Jones, and he had ambitions of starting a brewery. Someone shared the news with John Robbins Kimberly. The crusty Neenah pioneer was asked where he thought an appropriate site for the brewery might be. Kimberly thundered, "In hell, sir!" There is no telling if the story is true. If the Welshman Jones ever did manage to get his brewery going in Neenah, no record of it is known to have survived. The tale is probably apocryphal, but like any durable myth, there is a kernel of hard truth at its core. It tells of the conflict to come.

John Robbins Kimberly was a prominent member of Neenah's business community. He and most of his ilk were settlers from the East who had gone west to make their fortune. They were sober-minded and had little use for breweries or beer drinking. But to Kimberly's consternation, the village was attracting scores of folks of a more convivial nature. They brought their culture of pleasure with them. Among the newcomers was a brewer named Lachmann. To the Kimberly of legend, Lachmann would have represented the devil incarnate.

En route to Neenah, Jacob Lachmann faced obstacles tougher than John Robbins Kimberly. Lachmann was born about 1823 in Württemberg in southwest Germany. He was a man of his time. In his youth, Lachmann had followed in his father's footsteps and trained as a whitesmith but then abandoned the cutlery trade to apprentice as a brewer. In 1848, he joined the revolutionary fray in Europe, leading a company of "Free Troops" in the struggle for constitutional rights. It did not end well. In the backlash following the revolt, Lachmann was forced to flee his homeland. He arrived in New York in 1849 and spent the next several years traveling and working his way around the eastern United States. In 1854, the thirty-one-year-old went to Milwaukee. Two years later, he was in Neenah looking to set up a brewery.

On May 21, 1856, Lachmann purchased a large plot on the western shore of Little Lake Butte des Morts where it drops into the Neenah Slough. By the end of the year, he was producing beer there. Not surprisingly, his brewery looked like something lifted from the German countryside. Lachmann's two-story brick brewery near the water's edge was also home for himself, his wife and their young boy. They were far enough from the heart of the village to be out of the way but close enough to supply its beer. It was best not to draw more attention than necessary.

From the outset, Neenah was conflicted on the subject of alcohol. The Germans, Irish and Danes who had settled throughout the village loved their beer. Their Yankee neighbors did not. From the pulpits of their Protestant churches, the Yankees strove to set the moral tone for the emergent Neenah. Their influence was inescapable. They sought to make Neenah a dry town.

Looking down Wisconsin Avenue in Neenah, 1856.

Prior to Lachmann launching his brewery, newspaper reports on the development of Neenah make no mention of saloons there. But a decade later, the town of 2,300 people had eight licensed drinking establishments. Inevitably, ethnic tensions arose. It would stew for decades to come. The Yankees had their churches and rectitude. The immigrants had Lachmann's brewery and its beer. Neither side was giving in.

THE FOAMING FIFTH WARD

At the close of 1855, Oshkosh had two breweries. It required another. The Fifth Ward along the Fox River was building up. It now teemed with mills producing construction lumber and wood products from logs sent downstream out of camps in the Wolf River pineries. The mills attracted workers. The workers attracted brewers.

The first brewers in the Fifth Ward arrived in the fall of 1856. August Weist and Tobias Fischer were Germans. Weist was born in Arnsdorf in 1829; Fischer, born in 1812, was a Bavarian. Both had served apprenticeships in breweries in their homeland. Fisher left Germany for America in 1854, and Weist came two years later. When they reached Oshkosh, they formed a partnership. On October 13, 1856, Fischer and Weist bought an acre of land near the southwest corner of High and New York Avenues. Their plot was just off the Fox River, within earshot of the high whine issuing from Edwin Kellog's steam sawmill. Kellog was happy to have them there. He sold them the land and loaned them money to get started. Fischer and Weist set up shop in the heart of the Fifth Ward.

Launching a brewery in 1856 was not the ordeal it is today. There was little in the way of licensing or regulation to fight through. The most arduous task was the construction of the beer cellar. The brewery itself would have been composed of simple, wood-framed buildings, their vernacular architecture blending in with most other structures in the area. You would have hardly known it was a brewery if not for the blanketing aroma of boiling hops or the sharp off-gas of lager yeast in fermentation. The low barrier to entry made for a fluid situation. Brewers came and went on a whim. Fischer and Weist were a case in point. They had hardly settled in when Weist abandoned their operation. By August 1857, Weist was living in Princeton, Wisconsin, trying to get a brewery started there. Weist sold his share in the Oshkosh brewery to Fischer, who went looking for a new partner. By September, he had one. His name was Christian Kaehler

Of course, Kaehler came from Germany. It was almost a requirement for a brewer working in Oshkosh. Kaehler was born in 1833 and was twenty years younger than Fischer. Age wasn't the only thing separating them. Kaehler had come from Oldenburg, in northern Germany, where ale brewing had yet to be overwhelmed by the lager beer barrage. In America, Kaehler would leave the *alt* tradition behind—here he would brew lager. Kaehler could not have found a better mentor. The Bavarian Fischer had been making lager for almost as long as Kaehler had been alive.

They named their joint effort the Busch Brauerei. By early 1858, Fischer and Kaehler were already looking for a new location. They found what they wanted a couple blocks away near the southeast corner of Algoma Boulevard and Vine Avenue. Algoma Boulevard had become the Fifth Ward's main street. Fischer and Kaehler would be in the midst of its traffic. The new brewery with its taproom would provide a convenient stopping-off point for folks traveling along the boulevard.

By the end of April 1858, Fischer and Kaehler were settled in. They placed an ad in the *Oshkosh Deutsche Zeitung*, a German-language newspaper, inviting everyone to come to the brewery for a special beer.

> *This famous Salvator Beer, which was brewed on the coldest day of this winter, has now finished its lagering period and is to be tapped in our*

„Salvator Bier"

Oshkosh's Bier-durst'ge Seelen
Werden baldigst laut erzählen
Daß über Bachus Majestät
Gambrinus hoch erhaben steht!

Dieses berühmte Salvator Bier, welches
an dem kältesten Tage dieses Winters ein-
gebraut, hat nun seinen Ärgerungsprozeß
vollendet und soll künftigen Sonabend am
1. May — in unserer Brauerei angezapft
werden.

Wir laden alle Oshkosher ein uns in
unserer Busch Brauerei am Sonnabend und
die folgenden Tage zu besuchen und ver-
sprechen ihnen einen Genuß zu verschaffen,
wie es bisher noch nie dagewesen.

Kommt, kommt all zu

Fischer und Köhler.

Left: Salvator Bier at Fischer and Kaehler's Busch Brauerei, *Oshkosh Deutsche Zeitung*, May 5, 1858.

Below: From the *Oshkosh City Directory and Business Advertiser* for 1872 and 1873.

FIFTH WARD BREWERY,

CHRISTIAN KAEHLER, Prop.,

No. 166 Algoma Street,

OSHKOSH, - - - WISCONSIN.

brewery on the coming Saturday evening, the 1ˢᵗ of May. We invite all Oshkoshers to visit us on Saturday and the following days in our brewery, and we promise to give them a pleasure like never before. Come, come all to Fischer and Köhler.

Good as it sounds, it did not last. On October 19, 1858, Fischer sold his stake in the brewery to Kaehler. It was almost two years to the day since he and Weist had gotten underway. Fisher had blazed through two partners and two breweries in two years. He was now forty-six, but the road kept calling.

Fischer left for St. Louis, where he immediately involved himself in another new brewery.

Kaehler wasn't going anywhere. As production increased, he built up the brewery. Some eighty years later, a group of "old settlers" recalled Kaehler's plant. They said it was made up of several buildings accompanied by beer cellars "sunk low in the ground." The brewery itself was set back approximately two hundred feet from the street with a wide drive leading up to it from Algoma Boulevard. The entire complex was surrounded by a high board fence.

At the close of the 1850s, the Busch Brewery was flourishing, as was Kaehler. He and his wife, Louise, had started a family. Their first child was a son named William. They all lived at the brewery. Christian Kaehler was not yet thirty years old. In the New World, all things were possible.

THE BREWERY ON THE BUTTE

There's a good chance Christian Kaehler knew a man named Christoph Klenk. Brewers tend to keep up with fellow brewers in their vicinity. Klenk had launched a brewery in Winnebago County about the same time Kaehler was getting his going. The two men spoke the same language, literally and figuratively.

Christoph Klenk was born in 1816 in the German territory of Württemberg. Amidst the European revolutions of 1848, he left for America. He appears to have gone first to New Orleans and worked as a brewer there. In 1856, Klenk found his way to Winnebago County and the small village of Butte des Morts. Augustin Grignon may have had something to do with that. The old fur trader had launched the county's first approximation of a tavern back in 1818 and had become a tireless promoter of the village he founded. In 1848, Grignon established the original plat for the village of Butte des Morts, where he now ran a hotel. Grignon later petitioned the state to have the county seat moved from Oshkosh to his village. That was not going to happen. A brewery, on the other hand…

On January 20, 1857, the seventy-six-year-old Grignon sold two of his lots to Christoph Klenk. At the time, the village was home to fewer than eight hundred people. In 1850s Wisconsin, that was more than enough to keep a brewery going. By 1857, the state was already home to more than 140 breweries. Dozens of them were in rural communities. Any burg within

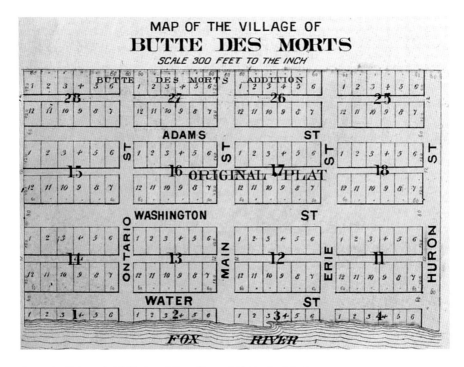

Augustin Grignon's 1848 plat of the village of Butte des Morts.

proximity of five hundred or so German immigrants found it could support a brewery. Butte des Morts fit the bill. Butte des Morts had something else in its favor: it was along a well-traveled route running from Green Bay to Portage. The flow of people through the village inspired the establishment of hotels and saloons. The saloon culture that began developing in Butte des Morts in the 1850s was outsized in comparison to the village's actual size. It was the kind of thing that would have caught the attention of a brewer scouting a location.

Christoph Klenk's attention would also have been drawn to the natural advantages of the site he intended to build on. The property he purchased was on a shallow bluff sloping down to the Fox River. Klenk could not have seen that hill without seeing himself tunneling a beer cellar into it. The ice required to cool his vault would be within easy reach—each winter, the river would give him all he needed. This was indeed a model location.

Klenk probably had the brewery in operation by the close of 1857. By 1858, he was definitely producing beer there. Klenk purchased more of the neighboring property from Grignon. The brewery came to occupy half the land south of Washington Street between Ontario and Main Streets. By the end of the decade, Klenk was producing about 250 barrels of beer annually, a healthy output for a rural brewery. The brewery on the hill became a landmark for travelers on the river and made for another reason to stop in Butte des Morts.

FLAVOR ALL THEIR OWN

In the ten years ending in 1859, ten separate breweries went into operation in Winnebago County. The growth within the industry mirrored that of Winnebago County as a whole. The county's population in 1850 was 10,179. By the end of the decade, it had more than doubled to 23,770. Much of the growth was concentrated in its two largest cities, Oshkosh (population 6,087) and Menasha (population 1,436).

By the mid-1850s, a full quarter of Winnebago County's residents were foreign-born. The majority of the immigrants came from Germany. The brewers among them arrived with a skill set making them uniquely suited to the rough-hewn life of the Wisconsin frontier. They were self-reliant in the extreme. They were maltsters, brewers, and coopers. They were able to build with their own hands most of what was needed to produce and package beer. Along the way, they established a beer culture that would grow exponentially in the decades to come.

Agriculture with brewers in mind developed in company with that culture. The early beers of Winnebago County were produced from locally grown barley malted at the brewery. By the 1850s, even hops could be sourced locally. Winnebago County's brewers and farmers were in the process of creating something unique to their region.

3

THE BITTER HARVEST

Hop Culture in Winnebago County

Winnebago County's early beers were composed of four essential ingredients: water, malted barley, hops and yeast. Good water was relatively easy to come by. A brewer could have all he needed after completing the backbreaking work of drilling a well. Barley was supplied by local farmers. Malting it at the brewery was time consuming and laborious, but shortages of the grain were rare. Yeast practically took care of itself. After the initial pitch was secured—usually passed along from another brewer—it would grow in abundance with each new batch of fermenting beer. A brewer would harvest what he needed and re-pitch it into the next brew. Then there were the hops. That could be a problem.

Hop farming is believed to have been underway in Wisconsin by 1837. More than a decade later, it reached Winnebago County. The first brews of Konrad, Schussler and Sperry required them to source their hops from hop merchants, most likely working out of Milwaukee. It was a dicey way of doing business. The green, cone-shaped flowers of the female hop plant are notoriously fragile. Their most vulnerable aspect—the pungent oils that lend beer its distinctive bitterness and aroma—is the first to degrade. A Winnebago County brewer ordering a bale of hops from a dealer in Milwaukee would have had little idea what he was getting until it arrived. Access to hops improved within a couple years of brewing being introduced to the county. By 1852, there was at least one wholesaler located in Oshkosh. A year later, the first substantial harvest of local hops took place on a small farm in Allenville in the town of Vinland. They were grown by the man who put the Allen in Allenville.

Silas Allen was born in 1813 in Sturbridge, Massachusetts. When he was thirteen, the Allen family relocated to Madison County, New York. Madison County was the leading producer of hops in the United States, and the Allen family farm contributed to that output. In 1847, Silas Allen set out on his own, heading west. He knew where he was going. The prime band for hop cultivation in the United States is along the forty-fifth parallel. Madison County straddles the forty-third parallel, while Winnebago County is located along the forty-fourth. Allen had not picked Winnebago County on a whim. According to family lore, when Silas Allen set out for Wisconsin, he brought a barrel of hop roots along with him on his wagon. Allen was a man on a mission.

Upon his arrival, Allen went on a land-buying spree. Beginning in February 1848, he purchased hundreds of acres of public land in Winnebago County from the U.S. Land Office in Green Bay, including more than a hundred acres in the town of Vinland. What came to be known as the Allen Estate was just west of County Road G and Hilltop Road. For centuries, that land had been hunting grounds for native tribes. Now it would grow flowers for beer.

Hop cultivation can be arduous. These are climbing plants requiring copious handwork. A grower must train the plant's vertical growth up ropes anchored in the ground and buoyed by a trellis. For Allen, that meant posting rows of twenty-foot oak poles in the earth—dozens of them. After the yard was prepared came more work and waiting. It could take two or three years for a hop yard to mature to the point of producing a harvest worthy of processing. By 1853, Allen's yard was bearing fruit. The *Oshkosh Courier* told of Allen's 1854 harvest. The paper reported, "His crop the last season from five acres of ground, was over 6,000 lbs." In 1853, farmers were getting 25¢ a pound for their hops. Allen got almost 40¢ a pound for his 1854 harvest. Off that five-acre plot, he made about $2,300 (approximately $70,000 in today's money). That caught the attention of other farmers. Hops had arrived in Winnebago County.

THE WOLF

Humulus lupulus is its more formal name, *lupulus* being Latin for "little wolf." The epithet is derived from its tendency to aggressively spread. In

Winnebago County, the plant lived up to its name. From the Allen farm, hop cultivation radiated outward. Following closely on Allen's heals was a farmer in Oshkosh named John Braley. Braley, like Allen, had come from a hop farming background back East, where he had grown hops in Vermont. In 1850, he reached Winnebago County, and in June that year, he purchased fifty-three acres on Algoma Boulevard across from Riverside Cemetery.

Braley's first harvest came in the late summer of 1854. Not to be outdone by Allen, he took a few strands from his yard to the offices of the *Oshkosh Courier*. The paper deemed them "very fine samples" and urged area farmers to pay heed. "[We] should think from the success which has attended MR. BRALEY'S efforts this season, that our farmers would do well to direct their attention to this matter." Did they ever: by the early 1860s, hopyards had been planted throughout the northern half of the county. The largest cluster crossed through the townships of Clayton, Vinland, Winchester and Winneconne. There, more than a dozen hopyards were under cultivation among the lands that stretch from State Road 76 west to Lake Winneconne. Most of those yards were ten acres or less.

Like the brewers who bought their crops, hop growers tended to have a shared pedigree. Many of Winnebago County's hop farms were started by Yankee settlers. Often they came from areas where hop culture was already well established. Their migration west proved timely—beginning in the 1860s, a series of blights, infestations and late frosts greatly diminished the yields of New England and New York. The downturn caused a spike in the

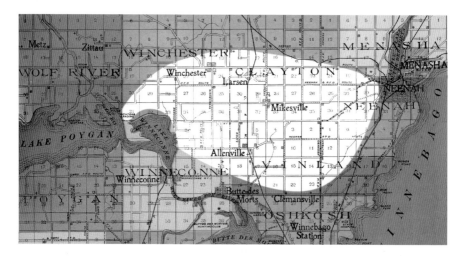

The lightly shaded area indicates Winnebago County's main hop belt in the 1860s.

Lorenzo Hinman's farm as it appeared in the late 1870s. His oast, with its conical roof, is the third building from the left.

price of hops. At the same time, Winnebago County's recently established yards were reaching maturity. The money came rolling in.

One of the farmers who grew wealthy on hops was Lorenzo Hinman. He had come to Wisconsin from Massachusetts, the last leg of his journey made behind a team of oxen. In 1848, Hinman purchased 360 acres of Winnebago County land spanning the townships of Clayton and Vinland. His hopyard went in near the northwest corner of Breezewood Lane and Center Road. In late summer, the Hinman yard became a destination for seasonal workers following the harvest.

In an age before mechanized hop picking, the work of harvesting was done by hand. A ten-acre hopyard could require fifty or more pickers. Attracting and managing that labor was a struggle. Timing was everything. The hops ripened at the end of August and at that point needed to be picked and dried as quickly as possible. Delays would impact the quality of the hops and the price a grower would receive for them. In the yards, the pickers worked in teams. The twenty-foot-high plants were cut down and the hops plucked off. The bright-green, thumb-sized cones were collected in wooden boxes three feet long. The pickers were led by a box tender responsible for ensuring the pickings remained free of leaves and stems. The harvest could last two weeks, sometimes longer.

Farmers assumed responsibility for housing, feeding and entertaining the pickers. Most of them were young people from neighboring communities. North of Lorenzo Hinman's farm in the town of Clayton was a hop farm operated by the Roblee family. Their pickers lodged in a frame house that served as a dormitory during the harvest. Women slept on one side of the house, men on the other.

The Allen farm typically employed twenty to twenty-five pickers each season. The count swelled to seventy-five for the bumper crop of 1865. That harvest lasted nearly a month with the pickers housed in a barn. They slept on mattresses filled with straw. When the day's work was done, the pickers gathered for their evening meal. There was often music and dancing. For some pickers, the harvest was something like a working holiday.

Meanwhile, the hops were processed. At Hinman's farm, he had a special barn called an oast for drying hops. Inside the barn, hop cones were spread out on a slatted floor. Beneath it was a large cast-iron stove. The stove's heat would drift up into the hops and out through a vent in the cone-shaped roof. When the hops were dried, they were swept down a hole in the floor into burlap sleeves. Each bale weighed approximately 180 pounds.

THE GHOST OF DELHI

Hops were the staple crop for the farms around Delhi, a forgotten village in the town of Rushford. Delhi sprang up in the late 1840s around Luke Laborde's trading post on the Fox River. Laborde was born in Green Bay in 1810. His father was among the early French Canadian fur traders who settled in the area. In 1846, Laborde came to Winnebago County. Like August Grignon in Butte des Morts, Laborde had big plans for a village he practically willed into existence. Originally known as Laborde's Landing, he had the village platted in 1849 as Delhi. Shortly after, Laborde placed an announcement in the *Oshkosh True Democrat* saying he would give away lots to anyone willing to come and build.

Delhi's early progress was steady though not overly robust. That changed with the arrival of hops. In the 1860s, with hop prices on the rise, Delhi became a boomtown. A network of hopyards rose up around the village. When the pickers came to town, the sleepy hamlet came to life. Delhi's lone hotel—a twenty-two-room inn named the American House—grew so crowded during the harvest that pickers had to sleep in the attic and in hallways. Much of the processing took place in the village itself. Delhi had three drying barns and a press for baling.

Even Luke Laborde got in on it. Historian Kate Alderson wrote that Laborde had "thirty or forty acres of hops and his own hop house for drying." That would have been an extraordinarily large hopyard for the period. His drying barn, said to be one hundred feet long, would have been commensurate with that scale of agriculture. If the depiction is accurate, Laborde's hop farm would likely have been the largest in the county.

After Delhi's hops were picked, dried and baled, they were shipped down the Fox River to Oshkosh. After Oshkosh, they could wind up almost anywhere. By the mid-1860s, Wisconsin-grown hops were considered on par with those of New York. The *American Journal of Pharmacy*'s 1871 report on the culture of hops in the United States noted that "The hop gardens of New York and Wisconsin; they give the greatest yield and are considered the very best." The hops coming from those gardens were now being exported as far as England. What began with a barrel of roots planted in Allenville now attracted the interest of brewers internationally.

In 1860, Winnebago County was the fourth largest grower of hops in the state with a harvest near seventeen thousand pounds. By 1865, output increased to sixty-seven thousand pounds. Out-of-state merchants began zeroing in on the annual crop. As the East Coast growers struggled, hop farmers in Winnebago County were courted by dealers based in New York and Philadelphia. They'd take all they could get. The Jacob Ruppert Brewery of New York City went so far as to send an agent to live in Oshkosh. Francis Ruppert was the brother of brewery founder Jacob Ruppert. In the late 1860s, Francis Ruppert relocated to Oshkosh in hopes of getting the jump on other hop buyers canvassing the area. The Ruppert brewery was then the eighth largest in America, producing ten times as much beer as all of Winnebago County's breweries combined. For growers, supplying the local breweries became an afterthought. It was a seller's market, and they made the most of it.

Demand sent prices soaring. In 1865, farmers were selling their hops at 48¢ a pound. Just two years later, a shrewd grower could get 70¢ a pound. The hop craze was on. Hopyards went up everywhere, even in residential areas. "Hereafter [hops] will constitute a very important item in the production of this county," predicted the *Daily Northwestern*. The *Island City Times* of Menasha remarked with astonishment that the county's farmers had access to the best wheat market in Wisconsin, yet they were foregoing that crop in favor of hops. "Now the whole people seem to be crazy on the hop question," the paper observed. The madness ran headlong into an uncompromising reality.

UPROOTED

By 1868, there were approximately 150 acres of land in Winnebago County under hop cultivation. And there were dozens of disappointed farmers tending that land. The 1868 crop was stunted by lousy growing conditions, and the yield was modest. The disappointment turned to dismay as news came in that New York's hopyards had rebounded. The market grew flooded with hops. Prices tanked. Formerly free-spending buyers now offered Winnebago County hop growers as little as a nickel a pound and sometimes less. Farmers who had bet the farm on the promise of quick riches were made instantly destitute. Delhi's hopyards were decimated. Some were able to get by—Lorenzo Hinman saw his net worth plummet, but he managed to hang onto his farm, as did the Allens and the Roblees.

Others were less fortunate. The fate of R.G. Freeman, a farmer in the town of Oshkosh, was typical of what became of those who entered the game too late. After returning from the Civil War, Freeman purchased a small farm with a loan he had taken for $2,000 (about $31,000 in today's money). Freeman went about building up a hopyard. It made sense: no other crop approached the profitability of hops. He figured one good harvest would bring in more than enough cash to satisfy his debt. Freeman's first crop ripened in the summer of 1868. He had planned on selling it for $3,000. He got $300. Freeman's bright plans lay in ruins. His farm was sold off in a lottery.

The crash of 1868 was the beginning of Winnebago County's retreat from hop culture. But there were also other forces at work. In 1867, Wisconsin's Methodist convention resolved to exert its influence upon farmers abetting the brewing trade by growing hops. The tactic fit neatly into the growing trend in support of alcohol prohibition in rural Winnebago County. Whether driven by simple economics or moral suasion, the outcome was the same. Farmers began uprooting their hopyards.

By 1876, hop acreage in Winnebago County had dipped nearly 10 percent. In the town of Rushford, where the great hopyards of Delhi had flowered, a mere eight acres remained under cultivation. The towns of Vinland and Clayton were more committed. Combined, the two townships still had over ninety acres given over to hops. But even they wouldn't hold on much longer. By the end of the 1870s, there were just thirty-three acres devoted to hops in all of Winnebago County. In a decade, production had dropped from more than 175,000 pounds to less than 25,000 pounds. By 1880, it was all but over. Winnebago County's once-thriving hop culture was erased. The distinctive barns constructed specifically for their task were broken down for scrap. Poles were pulled out of fields, which were taken over by corn and cows. At Hinman's farm, a thicket of those old hop poles rested like totems against a barn well into the 1930s. Even that was more than what remained of Delhi. The village receded after the hopyards went fallow. Harney's 1880 *History of Winnebago County* noted that Delhi had "long since depopulated."

Silas Allen was long gone, too. He died in 1859 from sunstroke while working in his field. His family carried on with the farm and raising hops. In 1880, a one-hundred-foot swath was cut through the last hopyard on the Allen farm when the Chicago & North Western Railway laid track there. That was the end of the Allen yard. Just a whisper of the old ways remains. More than 160 years after he brought his wagon west, hops still grow wild at the site of Silas Allen's yard. They're a perennial reminder of what once was.

4

1860-1879

A LOCAL FLAVOR

Charles Rahr was born in 1836 in Wesel, a city in North Rhine–Westphalia, Germany. The Rahrs had been brewing beer and vinegar there from time immemorial. Then came the 1840s and the beginning of the Rahr exodus. The first to go was Wilhelm Rahr, Charles Rahr's uncle. Wilhelm left Wesel in 1847. He went to Manitowoc, where he established one of Wisconsin's early lager breweries. This may have been something new in the Rahr line. Wesel had long been known for its dark ales, but the Rahrs left that in their homeland. In Wisconsin, the family name would be synonymous with lager beer.

After Wilhelm planted his flag, his nephews rallied. First came Henry Rahr, arriving in 1853. Henry worked in Manitowoc at his uncle's brewery for a few years then moved to Green Bay and established a brewery there with August Hochgreve. In 1856, Henry's brothers Charles and August made the voyage over. Each of them did stints at Wilhelm's Manitowoc brewery and Henry's Green Bay brewery. Charles went on to Davenport, Iowa, working in a brewery there for eighteen months before returning to Wisconsin. In the fall of 1861, he enlisted in the Ninth Wisconsin Volunteer Infantry, and he spent the next three years fighting in the Civil War.

He returned to Green Bay after mustering out of the army on December 3, 1864. At midnight on December 31, Charles Rahr married Caroline Hochgreve, a sister of Henry's partner August in the Green Bay brewery. Charles was twenty-eight now and looking to start his own brewery. Rowdy Oshkosh was just the place for him. On July 10, 1865, Charles purchased

Right: Charles Rahr.

Below: The Rahr Brewery in the 1880s.

five acres on the shore of Lake Winnebago. That summer, he and his brother August began building their brewery. Initial notices for the venture identify it as the City Brewery, Charles Rahr & Brother, proprietors. The urban inference pointed to the change afoot. The Rahr brewery was unlike the earlier frontier breweries. This brewery was larger, with an annual production capacity in excess of one thousand barrels. The Rahrs had an eye toward Oshkosh's growing saloon trade. That's where the "Brother" came in.

While Charles was in the brew house, August was out on the town selling and distributing beer. His was the face that came to be associated with the brewery. People began referring to it as August Rahr's Brewery. That was probably for the best—Charles could be less than endearing. He was quarrelsome and rough. He preferred to speak German. August was more amenable and friendlier. Together, they made a good team, and the experience they had gained in Green Bay and Manitowoc informed their approach.

This was not another village brewery predicated on selling buckets of beer to its neighbors. Those bucolic days were ending. Charles and August may not have realized it, but their brewery was the bellwether of change. Tradition was going to be peeled away layer by layer until something uniquely American emerged. The reordering would be inexorable and pitiless. Those who could not adapt would be crushed.

SCHWALM THE SAXON

In the 1860s, nobody had a better view into Winnebago County's brewing upheavals than Leonhardt Schwalm. He shows up almost everywhere. His influence was widespread and his legacy abiding. The Schwalm name would be associated with beer in the county for more than a century. Leonhardt Heinrich Reinhold Schwalm was born in 1827. The family home was in Saxony in eastern Germany, where the Schwalms were farmers. That was due to change. In the mid-1800s, the Schwalms began their migration. Leonhardt Schwalm left Germany in 1851; he was twenty-five and already a brewer.

The ship that brought Schwalm over docked in New York City on July 16, 1851. He went to Wisconsin and settled in the town of Nekimi in southern Winnebago County, where the Schwalm family was in the process of establishing its new farm. Initially, Schwalm seems to have occupied himself with farming. If he was involved in brewing, it was on a scale that escaped the attention of those inclined to make note of such things. Then again, farm breweries were hardly remarkable in 1850s rural Wisconsin. Schwalm could have been brewing up a storm.

His formal connection to beer and brewing in Winnebago County begins in 1858. In June of that year, he launched a "lager beer salon" on the south side of Oshkosh. Details of that operation are scarce, but there's an indication that some of the "excellent lager beer" Schwalm was serving may have been of his own creation. The saloon was merely a stepping stone.

In 1862, Schwalm met up with the freewheeling Anton Andrea of Oshkosh's Lake Brewery. Andrea, ever fickle in his pursuits, was turning away from his brewing business, and Schwalm stepped in. On June 23, 1865, he signed a three-year lease on the Lake Brewery. Almost fourteen years after arriving in America, Leonhardt Schwalm finally had a legitimate brewery on his hands. In fact, he may have had two.

On November 17, 1862, Christoph Klenk sold his brewery in Butte de Morts to Louis Schwalm, Leonhardt's older brother. There's no known record of Louis ever having worked as a brewer; his time as owner of the Butte de Morts brewery doesn't alter that. Louis owned the brewery, but he was making his living in Oshkosh, where he ran a saloon and liquor store. Louis was certainly selling beer, but it's unlikely he was making it. That chore probably fell to Leonhardt. Three years later, he owned the place.

In 1865, a series of transactions reshaped the brewing scene in Butte des Morts and Oshkosh. Leonhardt Schwalm played a role in all of them. First came his exit from the Lake Brewery. Schwalm's lease on that brewery was up in September, and he didn't renew it. On November 6, Schwalm bought the Butte des Morts Brewery from his brother. Just a few weeks later, Schwalm sold that brewery. By this time, he was already busy with another brewery. This one was in Oshkosh, in the part of town known as Brooklyn.

The Brooklyn Brewery

In the 1850s, a small community developed along the south bank of the Fox River in Oshkosh. Its geography reminded Yankee settlers of a particular New York City borough, so they called it Brooklyn, and the nickname stuck. Germans and Bohemians making their homes there adopted it as their own. When the first brewery was established on the south side of Oshkosh, it practically named itself.

On October 4, 1865, Leonhardt Schwalm set the Brooklyn Brewery in motion when he purchased land on Doty Street. The brewery would be about a half-mile south of Brooklyn's commercial district. A year in, Schwalm sold half his stake to August Horn, his brother-in-law. The Bavarian-born Horn wasn't a brewer, but he turned out to be a natural when it came to promotion. Horn was gregarious in the extreme. He was in his element when he was in a saloon. He liked to make the rounds, and he'd often pick up the tab for those drinking with him. People took to following

The first iteration of Horn and Schwalm's Brooklyn Brewery, built in 1866.

him around. Within Oshkosh's German community, he grew into something of a celebrity. His perambulations were sometimes covered by Oshkosh newspapers. They presented Horn in a gently comic tone that endeared him to those who otherwise had little affection for the beer-soaked ways of Oshkosh's immigrant population.

At times, the Brooklyn Brewery was home to as many as twenty people. Residents included brewery workers and both the Horn and Schwalm families. The workers would live one week with the Horns, the next with the Schwalms. For the children, making beer and the chores that went with it were part of daily life. Most of the sons would grow up to become brewers.

The cozy atmosphere belied the ambitions of Horn and Schwalm. After his terms at the Lake and Butte des Morts Breweries, Schwalm was intent on building this brewery into something more substantial. Horn struck deals with saloon keepers that kept their beer flowing in every part of Oshkosh. From there, they expanded outward, pushing their lager into Omro, Butte des Morts and Winneconne. The focus on distribution paid off. The Brooklyn Brewery grew into the largest in Winnebago County. By the end of 1872, production for the year had climbed to one thousand barrels. And then Leonhardt Schwalm died.

Schwalm was forty-five when he passed away unexpectedly on March 17, 1873. He left a wife and seven children. Schwalm's widow, Maria, and August Horn were now partners in a brewery without a brewmaster. The gap was filled in part by Schwalm's fifteen-year-old son Theodore and Horn's twelve-year-old son Henry. They had grown up in that brewery, and they were about to be tasked with running it. They would have their work cut out for them. Competition among Winnebago County's breweries was growing fierce.

GOING FOR BOGK

Nobody was feeling the pressure more acutely than Frederick Bogk, a German-born and -trained brewer who ran a liquor store in Oshkosh before coming to Butte des Morts. On December 13, 1865, Bogk purchased the Butte des Morts Brewery from Leonhardt Schwalm. At the time, things looked promising. The symbiotic relationship between the village and its brewery had developed unimpeded over the previous decade. The brewery was producing about three hundred barrels annually. The local market absorbed all of it.

Initially, Bogk did well, and he expanded the brewery. Butte des Morts historian George Overton wrote that Bogk "carried on an extensive traffic in beer." His early success didn't escape the attention of other brewers in the area. In the late 1860s, Bogk found himself fighting to hold his ground against outside breweries pushing into his territory. Brewers in Oshkosh, the Rahrs in particular, targeted Butte des Morts with a zeal that seemed excessive considering the size of its market. Bogk was in trouble. There was no effective way for him to compete with breweries two and three times the size of his.

Output began to fall. Bogk's production slumped to two hundred barrels in 1870. In 1872, it fell to just eighty-two barrels. It was too little to sustain the business. Bogk turned to making vinegar in addition to beer and gradually transitioned away from brewing. The last mention of Bogk working as a beer brewer is in the federal census of 1880. Thereafter, the big red building on the hill produced malt vinegar.

Bogk's wasn't the first Winnebago County brewery to fail, but it was the first to be forced out by competition from other breweries within the county. It wouldn't be the last time that happened.

MEISTER YAGER

The fate of Frederick Bogk and the Butte des Morts Brewery had been sealed when a new brewery went up in the village of Winneconne. Separated by just four miles, the two villages combined were home to fewer than two thousand people. Something was bound to give. There was a new brewer from Germany who was going to force the issue. His name was Theodore Yager. He was born in Baden-Württemberg in 1825. Yager had trained as a brewer before leaving his homeland for America in 1851. He roamed for several years before coming to Wisconsin in 1857. He first settled in Dodge County, where he married Katharina Henrich. In 1860, the thirty-five-year-old Yager and his eighteen-year-old bride moved to Winneconne.

Initially, Yager worked as a cooper in Winneconne. Barrel making was a skill in the repertoire of most German-trained brewers. But that business was short lived. On January 29, 1862, Yager enlisted in Company F of the Nineteenth Regiment of the Wisconsin Infantry and went off to fight in the Civil War. Yager was discharged as a second lieutenant in May 1864 and returned to Winneconne. He no doubt noticed the flurry of new breweries being launched in Winnebago County. If he was ever going have his own, now was the time.

On July 21, 1866, Yager bought two acres on the east bank of the Wolf River near the end of South First Avenue. The location was prototypical, with the river supplying all the winter ice he'd need to keep his lager caves cool. Yager built a wood-framed building to serve as his brew house, and by 1867, beer was flowing from the Winneconne Brewery.

The Winneconne Brewery was small, but Yager made the most of it. Within a few years, he was producing upwards of 400 barrels of beer annually. The output was impressive, especially when considering what Yager was working with. An 1870 assessment of the brewery indicates Yager was brewing frequently and in small batches. The mash was made in four wooden tubs of various sizes. Yager had 14 hogsheads—wooden barrels with a capacity of about 64 gallons—used for fermenting and aging his beer. He had 130 kegs for packaging the finished product. Yager, who still produced cooperage on the side, probably made every one of those tubs and barrels himself. It was a lean set up for a lager brewery. The lengthy aging time required for lager beer would have tied up his limited equipment, thereby limiting his output. Yager made ale to fill the gaps. The brewing process was much the same, but unlike the aged and mellow lagers, the more bitter and alcoholic ales were quick-turn beers made to be consumed fresh. By the 1870s, lager beer was

Winneconne Brewery.

Theodore Yager Prop.

—o—

L ager Beer, Ale and everything in the line made in the best manner, and furnished to customers at living rates. All kinds of tight barrel work done on short notice and upon reasonable terms.

From the *Winneconne Item*, December 2, 1871.

king in Winnebago County, but for brewers with less capacity, ale remained a necessity. It was also increasingly coming to be a sign of obsolescence.

Keeping up with the area's more productive breweries became a relentless scramble. What Yager had inflicted upon Bogk in Butte des Morts was about to be visited upon him. In the latter half of the 1870s, Yager began to struggle. The problem wasn't Neenah or Menasha. For the most part, breweries there kept to their own territory or, in the case of Loescher and Hall in Menasha, directed their surplus output north. The issue was Oshkosh. By 1878, Oshkosh had six breweries producing lager beer. The city's central location and access to waterways and railways made distribution into the rest of the county relatively easy. A brewer like Yager no longer had the benefit of isolation. Everything was now connected.

The Winneconne Brewery's output fell sharply. In 1878, Yager sold just seventy-eight barrels of beer. The next year's output of eighty-three barrels was equally disappointing. Meanwhile, there were breweries in Oshkosh producing well over one thousand barrels annually. They wielded their advantage. Small breweries saw their customers abandon them. Yager kept fighting it, but his days as a brewer were numbered.

BREWING ON THE ISLAND

In Menasha, Orville Hall and Frederick Loescher figured it out early: grow or go under. In 1856, they began to expand. Hall and Loescher abandoned their boxed-in brewery on River Street and relocated to their new, more expansive location at First and Manitowoc Streets. The timing was prescient. Hall and Loescher had cornered their market—Menasha, Neenah and Appleton were all theirs. Then, in 1856, Jacob Lachmann built his brewery in Neenah. In 1858, Appleton got its first brewery. But the newcomers hadn't caught them off guard. By 1860, Hall and Loescher were selling more beer than any other brewery in Winnebago County, with an output of six hundred barrels annually. Their ascendancy was not going to go unchallenged. A new set of rivals was arriving to lay the foundation for what would become Menasha's largest brewery.

The Island Brewery's beginnings were humble and to this day are obscure. Considering the success it would become, it's surprising how vague the origin story is. Most sources give the start date as 1860. Peter Caspary is said to have established the Island Brewery that year on the north side of Nicolet Boulevard where it meets Ahnaip Street. The 1860 date is cited in the 1901 publication *One Hundred Years of Brewing*, a seminal text on American brewing history. Time and again, that has been repeated as the brewery's date of origin. It's possible the brewery began then but unlikely. In 1860, Peter Caspary was just nineteen years old and living on a farm near Milwaukee.

By 1866, though, Peter Caspary had definitely arrived in Menasha with a plan to launch a brewery on Doty Island. The idea wasn't his alone. On June 21, 1866, he, his brother Simon and their brother-in-law Jacob Tuchscherer purchased an acre of land from Menasha banker Henry Hewitt. That plot would become home to the Island Brewery. The three men who built it went back a long way. Each was born in Germany, where their families held farms in the duchy of Nassau. Both families left Germany sometime around 1850 and settled on farms near one another in the town of Granville, north of Milwaukee. In the summer of 1858, Jacob Tuchscherer married the Caspary brothers' sister Regina. Tuchscherer had been living in Menasha for at least two years by then. The Caspary brothers, still on the family farm, were introduced to Menasha by Tuchscherer, who worked as a cooper there.

The location they picked for their brewery had a unique vantage point. It was next-door to St. Charles Borromeo Catholic Church (now St. Patrick's Catholic Church). It may have been an atypical place for a brewery, but it was also an opportune one. The church's congregation was predominantly

The Island Brewery, indicated by the arrow, as it appeared in the late 1860s.

of German and Irish descent—just the people the Caspary brothers and Tuchscherer would be courting. For the most part, the two institutions coexisted amiably. Shortly after the brewery was up and running, the parish built a school on its section of the grounds. People in Menasha came up with an epigram for the arrangement: Education, Salvation, Damnation.

Prior to launching the Island Brewery, neither the Caspary brothers or Tuchscherer had any notable brewing experience. That had become something of a trend among folks starting breweries in Menasha. Tuchscherer may have had at least some contact with the profession. He was an associate of Joseph Dudler and at one point lived nearby Hall and Loescher's brewery, where he might have been doing barrel work for them. The overall lack of experience was perhaps more of a problem than they realized.

The brewery was barely up and running before the Caspary brothers and Tuchscherer decided they'd rather do something else. On November 2, 1868, they sold the Island Brewery to another trio that included another team of German-born brothers, Joseph and Jacob "Fred" Mayer. The trio became a duo when Stephen Steubel, the third partner in the business, sold his stake back to the Mayer brothers two years after buying in. The Mayers were from Baden, Germany. Joseph, born there in 1840, was a year older than Jacob. Joseph was seven when the family left for America. The Mayer family settled on a farm just south of Milwaukee and, like their predecessors, there's no indication of either brother having been involved in brewing prior to purchasing the Island Brewery.

That wasn't the only factor working against them. The brewery itself was lacking. It was described as "tiny" and "cramped." An 1870 drawing of the facility shows a cluster of small buildings set back perhaps three hundred feet from Nicolet Boulevard. It wasn't much, but the Mayers did well with what they had.

Jacob Mayer proved to have a knack for selling beer. The brewery came to be associated with him. An 1872 advertisement for the Island Brewery mentions only Jacob's name. Joseph may have been less than pleased. It was rumored the brothers weren't getting along. In 1874, their partnership came undone. Jacob sold his interest to Joseph and moved to Neenah. Joseph Mayer now had the little brewery on the island to himself. Over the next five years, he worked it for all it was worth. By the end of the 1870s, he was selling more beer than either of his competitors in Neenah and Menasha. Mayer was getting plenty of unintentional help from the folks over on Manitowoc Street.

THE BEER BARONS OF MENASHA

By 1870, Orville Hall and Frederick Loescher had been working together almost fifteen years. The unlikely partners had been uncommonly successful, but now each was looking to move on. Hall was fifty-two. Loescher was a couple years younger. The difficult, mostly manual, labor of making beer was losing its allure. Though Loescher maintained his stake in the brewery, he had ceased tending to its day-to-day operations. A Bavarian-born cooper named John Lenz was there to fill in for him. Both Hall and Loescher wanted to sell out. The time had come.

On October 24, 1871, the brewery was purchased by a pair of German-born brewers who most recently had been making beer in Green Bay. When George Behre and Herman Merz were handed the keys, they were coming into what looked like a sure bet. They had taken ownership of an up-to-date, steam-powered brewery. Its campus stretched across six lots and was capable

The Menasha brewery as it appeared when George Behre and Herman Merz were its owners in the 1870s.

of producing three thousand barrels of beer annually. More importantly, the beer coming out of it was popular. When Behre and Merz arrived, the Manitowoc Street brewery was selling three times as much beer as the rival Island Brewery. Behre and Merz were looking to widen that gap.

The majority of their beer was sold locally, but that market was growing increasingly competitive. Behre and Merz began building up rural accounts. They kept two and sometimes three teams of horse-drawn wagons on the road delivering beer. They laid claim to areas of Winnebago and Outagamie County that were off the waterways and that couldn't be reached by railcar. The strategy was moderately successful.

By the mid-1870s, Behre and Merz were filling another role. They came to be seen as Menasha's local beer barons. There were dozens of such "regal" characters in beer-soaked Wisconsin. Most were knighted by journalists unable to resist a cliché. If a town had a brewery run by a personable brewer, some newspaper writer was bound to come along and declare it a fiefdom. Behre and Merz fit the bill perfectly. An article published in the July 27, 1876 *Winnebago County Press* captured them at peak stereotype.

The members of this firm are jolly, go ahead popular and business-like men hailing from the "Faderland." There is nothing "small" about either of them—this remark being—in a figurative sense especially applicable to that personification of Gambrinus, Mr. Herman Merz. This gentleman, one of the most affable and business-like men in Menasha, is securing a fair share of patronage. The quality of beer brewed by this firm will bear favorable comparison with that turned out by the celebrated Milwaukee breweries being brilliant in color and extremely palatable.

But the plaudits masked a less-pleasant reality. Behre and Merz had purchased the brewery for $10,000 (over $200,000 today). They borrowed heavily to do it. Their primary creditors were the former owners, Frederick Loescher and Orville Hall. In the interim, Hall had been elected mayor of Menasha. When Behre and Merz ran into financial trouble, they stopped making their payments to the mayor. This was not good. Behre and Merz had been blindsided by the unexpected rise of Joseph Mayer at the Island Brewery. At Behre and Merz, production flagged. Then, and at the worst possible time, George Behre died. He never even made it out of bed on Friday, September 13, 1878. His death was utterly unexpected. Behre was forty-seven years old.

It all fell apart after that. The hale and hearty Mr. Merz—the one compared to the beer deity Gambrinus—was no longer so warmly received. Hall and Loescher, among others, wanted their money. There was none to give. In the subsequent foreclosure proceedings, it was confirmed that the assets of the partnership had been exhausted. Merz relinquished the brewery. Menasha's beer barons had been dethroned.

The Trouble with Neenah

There were scores of people in Neenah pleased, no doubt, to see a local brewery fail. In the 1870s, these folks were banding together. They formed societies with sanctimonious names like the Crystal Lodge, the Good Templars and the Sons of Temperance. Their memberships ran into the hundreds. Their common goal was a ban on the sale of alcohol in the city of Neenah.

Then there were those other people. They had social clubs, too. Their meetings were more frequent and less formal. Their club names were just as indicative, but not so lofty—Sturm's, Herziger's, Pingel's, Paepke's. Neenah's saloon culture grew in tandem with the growing agitation for its abolishment. It existed as a counterculture set off from the city's dominant class and its Yankee values. You had to be in the know to know it was there.

Prior to the 1880s, newspapers serving both Neenah and Menasha presented Neenah as if it were a dry town. The city's brewery and saloons were rarely mentioned. Advertisements for alcohol adhered to a protocol. The "pure wines and liquors" being offered were always and exclusively "for medicinal purposes" only. It was nothing more than pretense, but the pretense had its effect. Jacob Lachmann could attest to that.

By 1870, Lachmann's Neenah Brewery was selling four hundred barrels of beer annually, not bad for a brewery serving a city of 2,600 people. Still, he could have been doing better. Over in Menasha—a slightly smaller city— there were two breweries that together were selling three times as much beer as Lachmann did. Menasha had its prohibitionists too, but not like Neenah's. In Neenah, their influence was pervasive. There was only one way to escape it.

On October 28, 1872, Lachmann sold the Neenah Brewery for $6,000. A few years earlier, the Mayer brothers had paid $9,000 for the similarly equipped Island Brewery in Menasha. It was all about location. The new brewer in Neenah was named Frank Ehrgott. He was a German immigrant who had come to Wisconsin by way of Pennsylvania. The $6,000 he paid for the brewery was about all he had. A month later, he borrowed $1,000 from Lachmann to keep himself going. Ehrgott needed more help. In 1874, he sold half his stake in the brewery to his brother Adam.

Frank Ehrgott. *Courtesy of Gwen Hinzman Sargeant.*

For the remainder of the 1870s, the Ehrgott brothers carried forth in much the same manner Lachmann had. The out-of-the-way brewery held its own. Its output was limited but steady. As the decade came to a close, though, it was growing increasingly clear that something had to change. Neither Lachmann nor the Ehrgott brothers ever managed to gain the upper hand in their local market. Now there was beer flowing into Neenah from every direction. The temperance troopers couldn't stop it. In the coming decade, Frank and Adam Ehrgott would see if they could.

IF IT WASN'T FOR BAD LUCK...

Down in Oshkosh, George Loescher was learning what encroachment was all about. When he launched the Oshkosh Brewery in 1852, he was the one who had come charging in. He and his brother Frederick planted their brewery just down the street from Jacob Konrad's Lake Brewery. Now the courtesy had been returned. By 1870, Loescher's brewery was the smallest of the six lager breweries operating in Oshkosh. This was going to be a tough decade all the way around. It got off to a terrible start.

On Sunday, October 8, 1871, some 300 people died in the Great Chicago Fire. That same evening, more than 1,500 were killed in the Peshtigo, Wisconsin fire. After George Loescher read of the devastation in the Monday afternoon newspaper, he might have felt a little more fortunate than he had all day. While those fires raged, his brewery had also been burning. The fire started about 4:30 p.m. in a barn connected to the brewery. It spread quickly, engulfing the entire complex. The property, valued at over $7,000, was a total loss. Loescher was insured for less than half its worth. If he rebuilt, he'd have to come up with the rest himself. He rebuilt.

The following spring, Loescher had his brewery running again. The new facility included a saloon. For a small brewer, an on-premise saloon could make all the difference—it could be enough to sustain the business. In this case, the arrangement may have been a little too convenient. It was well known George Loescher liked to drink.

Maybe it was the drinking, or maybe it was that he was fifty-three and tired of the daily grind. Whatever the reason, Loescher withdrew. In April 1872, he leased his new brewery to his eighteen-year-old son Leonard and

Oshkosh Brewery.

GEO. LOSCHER,

MALSTER,

AND MANUFACTURER OF

Ale and Lager Beer,

No. 90 River Street,

OSHKOSH, - - - WISCONSIN.

An advertisement from the *Oshkosh City Directory and Business Advertiser* for 1868 and 1869 with Loescher's last name spelled incorrectly.

a fifty-one-year-old railroad hand named Andrew Ackerman. It was an unusual pairing, and it didn't work out. The lease was for five years, but George Loescher was back to running the brewery well before those five years were up.

Then it happened again. And again, it was on a Sunday. On April 28, 1878, Loescher's brewery burned. It wasn't a total loss: the saloon was saved. A newspaper report from September that year tells of a seventy-nine-year-old Oshkosh man who spent the afternoon there and then drowned himself in the river a few hundred feet away. If Loescher had plans to rebuild, he canceled them then. It was as if the place was cursed. Loescher wasn't done yet, but he was done there.

A HARD PLACE

In 1865, Leonhardt Schwalm gave up his lease on the Lake Brewery in Oshkosh to launch his new brewery on the Brooklyn side of town. Immediately after Schwalm left, the brewery's owner, Anton Andrea, found a new man to take the place over. A butcher by trade, German-born Gottlieb Ecke was going to try his hand at making lager beer. In the fall of 1865, Ecke moved his family from their comfortable home in Stevens Point into a run-down brewery in Oshkosh. It was the kind of thing that made people shake their heads. A Fond du Lac journalist of the period wrote of Oshkosh, "This is a hard town to write about, because if you tell the truth you have to write hard things." The same could be said of Gottlieb Ecke.

The brewery Ecke took over was nothing to write home about. It was Oshkosh's first brewery, built in 1849. By 1865, it looked the part. The brewery was small, ill-equipped and conceived to meet the needs of an era that had passed. Initially, Ecke had a partner working with him, a man named Edward Becker. He wasn't long for this kind of thing. Within the year, Becker returned to Stevens Point. Ecke must have liked it well enough. A year into the lease, he bought the brewery outright.

Ecke did well. Success fueled his ambition. The little old brewery would never hold him. When Ecke acquired the property from Andrea, he also purchased several nearby lots on Harney Avenue. In 1868, Ecke began construction of a new brewery there, a larger brewery capable of outputting three thousand barrels of beer a year. It took him about a year to get the new place into production.

Charlotte Ecke.

He had come out of nowhere, but by 1870, Ecke was producing six hundred barrels a year and running one of the best-selling breweries in Winnebago County. There was a feverish quality to his approach. He burned hard and burned out. Gottlieb Ecke died suddenly on Sunday night, November 19, 1871. His body was discovered the following day. Ecke was thirty-seven years old. The circumstances surrounding his death were peculiar. There had been no reports of illness. His passing went almost entirely unreported, save for a fourteen-word obituary in the *Oshkosh Times*. The notice didn't even give his full name. Descendants later suggested it was a suicide. It ran in the family. Ecke's will lends credence to their suspicions. He signed it the day he died. Ecke left a wife and four young children. Charlotte Ecke inherited a new brewery and the insurmountable debt her husband had amassed to build it.

Charlotte Ecke wasn't the first woman in Winnebago County to own a brewery—that would be Regina Loescher. In 1859, George Loescher had put the title of the Oshkosh Brewery in his wife's name, but that had nothing to do with operational oversight. It was a piece of Loescher's fiscal chicanery. Charlotte Ecke's circumstance was something else entirely. She truly was the head of this brewery. Among the first things she did was find a brewer. She brought on Philip Neumann, a brother-in-law who, like Gottlieb before him, had been working as a butcher in Stevens Point. But Neumann's transition from meat to malt wasn't so seamless. Without Gottlieb Ecke's manic ambition, the brewery fell on hard times. Unable to service the debt she had inherited, Charlotte Ecke's brewery went into foreclosure. She enlisted her brother, Oshkosh carpenter Henry Timm, for help. When the foreclosure led to a sheriff's sale in 1874, Timm bought the property.

The struggle went on. Ecke's thirteen-year-old son, Otto, left school and went to work in the brewery. Otto would later commit suicide. The endeavor was hopeless. In the summer of 1875, Charlotte put an end to it and dissolved her partnership with Neumann. She posted notices in German that the brewery was available for lease or sale. In Stevens Point, Louis Ecke was feeling the pull of the city that had ruined his brother.

THE BOHEMIAN

Louis Ecke ran a saloon in Stevens Point before coming to Oshkosh in the fall of 1875. He knew how to sell beer but didn't know a thing about making it. The man he brought with him would take care of that. He was a Bohemian-born and -trained brewmaster named Lorenz Kuenzl. In some respects, Kuenzl would be Winnebago County's first modern brewer. The European-trained brewers who established the county's beer culture were schooled in methodologies that were centuries old. Kuenzl came up at a transition point. He came of age at a time when the older, darker beers were being supplanted by a new, golden beer called pilsner.

Kuenzl was born in 1845 in Bohemia in the village of Abtsroth, about one hundred miles northwest of Pilsen. The first pilsner had been brewed there three years before Kuenzl's birth. When Kuenzl began his brewing apprenticeship, this new beer was coming into vogue. Its popularity would shape him as a brewer and the beer he would make popular in Winnebago County. In 1871, Kuenzl left Bohemia for America. He settled in Stevens Point, where he became the brewmaster at the Lutz Brewery, the forerunner to today's Stevens Point Brewery. Kuenzl left that post in 1875, when Louis Ecke persuaded him to move to Oshkosh. By September, Kuenzl was making beer in the brewery Gottlieb Ecke had built.

The memory of his brother may have been more haunting than Louis Ecke cared for. He spent less than six months in Oshkosh before returning to Stevens Point. But Kuenzl wasn't going anywhere. He took over the brewery and took on a new partner, his wife's brother John Walter. After five years of disarray and stagnation, the big brewery on Harney Avenue was up and running again. Kuenzl was just getting started.

Lorenz Kuenzl and family around 1883.

A FARM BREWERY

While everyone else was going big, Franz Wahle was going his own way. For the past decade, he had been co-owner and then owner of what is now Stevens Point Brewery. Wahle had taken the sensible path. He built up his brewery's output and distributed his beer beyond his home base to increase sales and profit. He had done everything a smart brewer in the 1860s was supposed to do. He wasn't going to do that anymore. Wahle was forty-one years old when he sold his brewery to Andrew Lutz and headed for Oshkosh. On September 23, 1867, Wahle moved with his family to a forty-eight-acre farm at the south end of Doty Avenue. It was the real thing—a span of horses, a cow, fifteen sheep, two hogs, a cornfield, an apple grove and a vineyard. Why not a brewery? Wahle took care of that.

With the help of his brother Adolph, Wahle built a small brewery at the northern end of the property. It may have had sentimental value more than anything else. Wahle was born in northern Germany and trained as a brewer there. His farm brewery had to have reminded him of the rural breweries he spent time in before coming to America in 1854. There's no known surviving record of what Wahle was up to in his new brewery. There is indication of it being operational but nothing explicit about his beer or where it might have been going. That's not altogether unusual for breweries such as this. The fog recedes in 1869, after Wahle leased his brewery to two well-traveled brewers looking to leave Milwaukee.

The leader of the duo was John Glatz, born in Baden, Germany, on Christmas Eve, 1829. When Glatz was fourteen, he moved away from his family and into a brewery to begin his apprenticeship. When he was twenty-four, he left Germany and took his skills to America. He brewed in Cincinnati and Philadelphia before hitting Milwaukee, where his star rose, in 1857.

Glatz settled in at Charles T. Melms's South Side Brewery. It was then among the largest breweries in America. Glatz became its brewmaster. All was well until Melms died in 1869. Almost immediately, the brewery imploded. At that point, Glatz could probably have had his choice of jobs at most any brewery in Milwaukee. A cantankerous man, Glatz decided Oshkosh was more his style. In September 1869, Glatz moved his family into Wahle's Brewery. The following spring, they were joined by Christian Elser, the brother of Glatz's wife. Elser was also a formidable brewer. Before coming to Oshkosh, he had been making beer at Franz Falk's Bavaria Brewery, then among the largest of Milwaukee's breweries. For two brewers acquainted with the industrial-sized breweries of Milwaukee, the little brewery at the

The Union Brewery in the 1880s.

end of a sheep field must have been rather quaint. Perhaps, like Wahle, they were seeking an alternative.

The placid scene turned out to be a little too laid back for a man like Glatz. The break came on a frozen night in December 1871, when the brewery burned to the ground. Wahle had no insurance on the brewery. Glatz and Elser did but for less than half its worth. Between the brewery and their own assets, Glatz and Elser were staring down a loss of about $10,000 (over $200,000 today). These were not rich men. Having accidentally destroyed a brewery they didn't own, Glatz and Elser scrambled to raise funds. Within three weeks, they had what they needed. On January 10, 1872, they purchased two acres and the ruined brewery from Wahle. In the spring, they began rebuilding. There was nothing humble about this one—it would become a full-on production brewery, the largest in the county with a five-thousand-barrel annual capacity.

They called it the Union Brewery. A union it was. Elser was sixteen years younger than Glatz and much more affable, the nostrum to his acerbic partner. Glatz was argumentative and proud; he'd give no ground.

Somehow the union worked. While Glatz tended to the beer, Elser tended to the saloons buying it. Post-fire, the brewery grew at a rapid clip. By the end of 1878, the Union Brewery was outpacing every other in Winnebago County. The only brewery that came close to presenting a challenge was the Brooklyn Brewery, run by Horn and Schwalm a few blocks north on Doty Street. But things kept breaking in favor of Glatz and Elser. On March 29, 1879, the Brooklyn Brewery burned to the ground. Glatz and Elser didn't hesitate in exploiting the misfortune.

Production at the Union Brewery ratcheted up. In addition to selling kegged beer to saloons, Glatz and Elser were now offering bottled beer. In 1878, the Union Brewery became one of the first in Winnebago County to bottle its own beer. Glatz and Elser were going after a market they hadn't yet been able to reach. Most of their beer was being sold in Oshkosh saloons. There were more than forty of them now. The quantities of beer they dispensed was legendary, but those places weren't for everybody.

A majority of local residents wouldn't set foot in an Oshkosh saloon. That included any woman with any concern for her reputation. Glatz and Elser wanted to reach those people. To do so, they made an arrangement with a Main Street merchant named William Dichmann. The Union Brewery would distribute its bottled product through Dichmann's store. Dichmann even offered discreet delivery for those who didn't want to be seen walking onto Main Street with a package of beer. By November 1879, the Union Brewery's bottled beer had grown so popular that Glatz and Elser split the business in two: Glatz took over the brewery, while Elser took on the bottling trade. Each had become wealthy beyond expectation. From the ashes of the 1871 fire had risen Winnebago County's leading brewery.

WHITE BEER

Amidst the advances and expansions came something from the past—a beer both refined and rustic. The exceptionally pale style of cloudy and tart ale called white beer originated in sixteenth-century Europe. There were numerous interpretations. American brewers took their cues from the *weiss*, or white, beers of Berlin. Like brewers everywhere, though, the Americans put their own spin on it. In Europe, white beers were usually brewed with a large proportion of wheat. American brewers of the nineteenth century favored corn grits in place of wheat. The final product

A clay bottle from Leonard Schiffmann's brewery. The brewer's last name, stamped into the bottle, is spelled incorrectly.

was light bodied, highly effervescent, low in alcohol, slightly sour and extremely refreshing.

In Winnebago County, white beer began its rise in the 1870s. Oshkosh was the jumping-off point. The first mention of white beer comes in 1876, when both Leonard Schiffmann and Leonard Arnold were producing beer from separate breweries on the south side of Oshkosh. Both appear to have been making white beer. Schiffmann's operation may have begun first.

Leonard Schiffmann had been kicking around the Oshkosh beer scene for years. Born in Germany in 1819, he had reached Oshkosh in the early 1860s. By 1865, he was running a saloon on North Main Street. Schiffmann may have already been making white beer at this point. Because of its low strength—typically less than 3 percent alcohol by volume, or ABV—white beer was not taxed as an alcoholic beverage. The lack of regulation meant such breweries could exist without leaving a record. Luckily, Schiffmann left a few clues. Several bottles from the Schiffmann brewery have survived. Schiffmann may, in fact, have been the first brewer in Winnebago County to bottle beer. The clay bottles he used were favored by early white beer brewers because they were stronger than glass. Within those bottles, the beer underwent a secondary fermentation that created enough pressure to make most glass bottles explode. To hold the effervescence, white beer bottles used corks strapped in with wire. The surviving Schiffmann bottles are all of this type.

In the early 1870s, Schiffmann had more than his share of hardship. In 1872, his son Leonard Jr. died after falling into a vat of boiling wort at Horn and Schwalm's Brewery. In 1874, Schiffmann's North Main Street saloon was destroyed by fire. He moved to the south side. After 1875, Schiffmann lived and brewed on the west side of Doty Street just south of Eighteenth Avenue. His son Andrew, a former brewer at Horn and Schwalm's Brewery, was his partner. It didn't last long. By 1883, Schiffmann's Brewery was no more.

Leonard Arnold's term was similarly short. He began building up his brewery in 1875 after purchasing a lot at the southeast corner of Sixteenth and South Main Streets in Oshkosh. Arnold was somewhat typical of white beer brewers in that he also made vinegar. By 1881, his brewery was producing nothing but vinegar. Arnold sold the brewery to his brother George Arnold, who went on making vinegar there for decades.

Frederick Voelkel was another 1870s brewer of white beer in Oshkosh. Voelkel ran a saloon on Doty Street not far from Horn and Schwalm's Brewery. He may have been making white beer there as early as 1870. By the mid-1870s, he was definitely brewing it. Voelkel brewed white beer on and off into the 1880s.

In the 1880s, the small brewers of white beer in Winnebago County were displaced as larger breweries in Oshkosh and Menasha took up the style. It was also being sent in from Milwaukee breweries specializing in the product. The small, home-based brewers faded, but white beer remained. The tart, snappy ale remained a popular repast in Winnebago County well into the 1900s.

THE OLD ARTICLE

The twenty-year span ending with 1879 was the most frenetic in the history of brewing in Winnebago County. No fewer than fifteen breweries made beer in the county during this period. There may have been even more. Take, for example, Rudolph Otten. A stray tax record from May 1865 shows that Rudolph Otten of Oshkosh declared making 14.25 barrels of lager beer that month. It's the one and only known mention of this man being a brewer. Rudolph Otten was a Bavarian immigrant living on Oxford Street in Oshkosh. His brewery was probably home-based, producing small batches for a handful of customers. Most excise-tax records relating to beer from this period are thought to have been lost. How many Rudolph Ottens haunt those missing assessments?

Brewing in Winnebago County began with neighborhood and village breweries. By the end of the 1870s, that scenario had run its course. Larger breweries had come to dominate. The production numbers of 1878 tell the story:

Glatz and Elser's Union Brewery (Oshkosh): 1,530 barrels
Horn and Schwalm's Brooklyn Brewery (Oshkosh): 1,366 barrels
Mayer's Island Brewery (Menasha): 1,095 barrels
Merz and Behre (Menasha): 868 barrels
Kuenzl's Gambrinus Brewery (Oshkosh): 470 barrels
Ehrgott Brothers' Neenah Brewery (Neenah): 410 barrels
Rahr's City Brewery (Oshkosh): 340 barrels
Kaehler's Fifth Ward Brewery (Oshkosh): 140 barrels
Bogk's Butte des Morts Brewery: Unreported
Loescher's Oshkosh Brewery: Unreported
Yager's Winneconne Brewery: Unreported

The top five survived. Only one among the bottom five did. The scale of the breweries wasn't the only change. The beer itself was different. Locally grown hops were no longer in use. And new ingredients—corn and rice—had been introduced. Former Oshkosh brewer Joseph Schussler reminisced about the early years in an interview he gave at the turn of the century. Schussler claimed the beer produced then was better than any on the market in 1898. He told the reporter he had never enjoyed a glass of beer like the old article made in the early years. Schussler wasn't the only old-time brewer to make such claims. We'll just have to take their word for it.

5

THE BATTLE WITH THE BOTTLE

WINNEBAGO COUNTY'S BEER BOTTLERS

If you wanted to drink beer at home, your choices were limited. You could go to a brewery and take home a keg, but there were no kegerators in those days. Once tapped, you needed to keep at that barrel until it was drained. If that was too much, you could go to a saloon and get carryout. Most places would fill a bucket with beer. The standard "growler" or "can" was a galvanized pail that held two quarts. Again, though, you had to drink it right away.

Prior to the late 1870s, bottled beer in Winnebago County was a novelty. It was around, but it was expensive, rare and unreliable. Poor sanitation and no pasteurization resulted in a product that was often sour and turbid. Few brewers wanted anything to do with it. Byzantine regulations scared off many of them. Before beer could be bottled it had to be kegged, bunged and have tax stamps affixed. Then the kegs had to be removed from the brewery to an alternate location. Only then could the beer inside the kegs be bottled. The next step was even worse. The bottling process was slow and sloppy. It was accomplished with a thin rubber hose and copious waste. Getting the beer into the bottle was just half the battle. Corking the bottle to preserve carbonation was practically an art form. It usually involved a porcelain stopper with a rubber gasket and a wire bail. For most brewers, bottling beer was too burdensome to bother with. But there were others willing to do it. Beginning in the late 1870s, a host of independent bottlers went into business in Winnebago County. The early bottlers were often saloon keepers or moonlighting brewery employees.

They set up makeshift bottling plants in their saloons, homes or barns. Frank Lutz was among the first.

Lutz worked as a delivery driver for Glatz's Union Brewery and also ran a saloon. He started his bottling operation in the early 1880s. There was nothing special about his arrangement. It all took place at his bar on the south side of Oshkosh. What came out of there bore little similarity to the standard twelve-ounce bottles we're familiar with today. The Lutz bottles were amber yellow. Collectors describe the color as "old amber." And they were big. The laboriousness of the task could be somewhat diminished by putting more beer into fewer bottles. Lutz's bottles held a quart; they were called "picnic" sized. The bulbous blobbed lip encouraged you to pour the contents into a glass. The face of the bottle was embossed with "F. LUTZ OSHKOSH WIS." The indelible label increased the chance of the bottle finding its way back to his shop for another fill.

Independent bottlers grew in number as bottled beer grew in popularity. Oshkosh was the hub for it in Winnebago County. More than a dozen bottling works were established there before the turn of the century. Most of the bottlers were allied to a particular brewery.

In Menasha, Bernard Kasel began bottling beer in the 1880s. Kasel ran a saloon and *Somer Garten* at Appleton and First Streets. Both his bottling efforts and his saloon were tied to Milwaukee's Miller Brewing. For barmen like Kasel, selling takeaway bottled beer was more lucrative than selling beer by the pail. Customers expected to pay no more than a nickel to get their

In the 1880s and 1890s, Schlitz Brewing employed numerous bottlers in Oshkosh.

Among Jacob Mayer's prime accounts was the Murer House Saloon at 432 Sherry Street in Neenah. Built in 1892, the saloon was tied to Miller Brewing.

two-quart growler filled. Kasel could charge twice that, sometimes more, for a quart of his bottled beer.

Nobody worked the system like Jacob "Fred" Mayer. The former co-owner of Menasha's Island Brewery began bottling beer in Neenah in the 1880s. He established a bottling plant at Sherry and Union Streets, across the tracks from the Wisconsin Central Railroad station. Being so close to the depot was perfect. Mayer had contracts with Miller Brewing and Watertown's Hartig & Manz Brewery. They'd send kegs of beer by rail to Neenah. Mayer would take it from there. Some of the kegs he distributed to area saloons. Some kegs he drained into bottles. Mayer hired two drivers to make the rounds. They'd deliver the kegs to bars and sell bottles of beer on the street off their wagons. They were, in essence, rolling saloons. Mayer undercut everybody. He'd sell kegs of his "foreign" beer well below the going rate. When the local breweries complained, saloon keepers pledged to remain faithful to their product. Then they turned around and bought cheap beer from Mayer.

Over at the Island Brewery, they were throwing fits. The brewery took its grievances to Neenah's notoriously dry-aligned city officials, claiming Mayer engaged in illegal practices on behalf of Miller Brewing. Mayer was arrested and charged with selling beer without a license. Miller turned around and sued the Island Brewery for stealing its kegs. The case against the Island Brewery was dismissed. The case against Miller and Mayer eventually reached the Wisconsin State Supreme Court. In the end, Mayer would have to buy a license. In the meantime, he operated with impunity. Mayer bragged to a newspaper reporter that his sales had nearly doubled.

In the latter half of the 1890s, independents like Mayer began closing up their bottling shops. Advances in bottling equipment and changes in tax law incentivized brewers to take their bottling in-house. The old, embossed bottles bearing the names of independent bottlers are now highly sought-after collector's items. They are the fragile souvenirs of a brief era all but forgotten.

6

1880–1899

THE SHAKEOUT

T he 1880s began with a frenzy. By mid-decade, a wholesale reshuffling of Winnebago County's breweries had occurred. Some were lost along the way.

Christian Kaehler's Fifth Ward Brewery in Oshkosh was the first to go. His brewery was now twenty-three years old. What was charming in 1860 was a relic in 1880. Annual production had slumped well below two hundred barrels. Kaehler could no longer service the loans he had taken against the property. His creditors sued him. By the end of 1880, Kaehler had ceased production. He lost his brewery the following summer. In the spring of 1882, Kaehler's Fifth Ward Brewery was dismantled.

Theodore Yager in Winneconne was faring no better. The competition wasn't the only thing hounding him. The forests along the Wolf River had been decimated. Winneconne's dependence upon the resource left the village economy in ruins. Businesses of all types failed. People began moving away. Yager wasn't going anywhere. His brewery wasn't either. The Winneconne Brewery sputtered along, running on fumes. Production fell to less than one hundred barrels annually. By 1885, there were none at all. Yager opened a general store in Winneconne but still owned the idle brewery when it burned to the ground on the morning of June 25, 1893.

In Neenah, the Ehrgott brothers were trying to figure out how to avoid going the way of Kaehler and Yager. Like their breweries, the Neenah Brewery was old and surrounded by aggressive competitors. Instead of risking money on brewery expansion, the Ehrgotts took a different tact.

Frank Ehrgott purchased a new building at 128 West Wisconsin Avenue in Neenah. It was two stories, brick and perfect for a saloon. Frank and his wife, Clara, moved into the upper apartments. By the summer of 1880, they were pouring beer in the space below. The saloon anchored the brewery. It was the one place where the Ehrgott brothers need not worry about competition. If you were in Frank Ehrgott's saloon, you were drinking the Ehrgott brothers' beer. For now, at least, it was the bulwark they needed to sustain the brewery.

At the Island Brewery in Menasha, no half-measures were being taken. At the close of 1879, Joseph Mayer sold the brewery to George Habermehl, a brewer from New York City. Habermehl immediately moved to Menasha. He arrived to find a wanting facility that had somehow managed to become the most productive brewery in Neenah and Menasha. Habermehl wasn't taking that position for granted. He undertook an aggressive expansion program. In the fall of 1880, the *Menasha Press* reported, "This firm is an enterprising one and does not believe in selling down and piling away riches while conducting a thriving business."

That was probably the last thing Werner Winz wanted to read. While Habermehl was building up, Winz was moving into the failed brewery last operated by Merz and Behre at Manitowoc and First Streets. Winz was undaunted. He knew how fast things could change. He'd been in the beer business for decades. His career was filled with impulsive twists. Werner Winz was born in Germany in 1841. He began his training as a brewer there after quitting school at age eleven. Winz quit Germany in 1868. He went to Wisconsin and found work in Milwaukee as a maltster at Schlitz. In 1871, he moved to Appleton, and a year later, he relocated to Menasha. There Winz met up with Joseph Mayer and went to work at the Island Brewery. In 1876, Winz returned to Appleton and purchased a half-interest in what would become George Walter's Star Brewery. In 1880, he sold out, moved back to Menasha and bought the brewery at Manitowoc and First Streets. The German whirlwind had finally found a home.

The scene was just as hectic in Oshkosh, especially at Horn and Schwalm's Brooklyn Brewery. On March 29, 1879, the Brooklyn Brewery burned to the ground after a small fire in the brew house grew into a conflagration. The loss was total. For the better part of a year, the brewery was out of commission. But what rose from the ash was more than a brewery, it was a new way of doing business. The rebuilt Brooklyn Brewery was the largest, most technically advanced brewery in Winnebago County. Constructed entirely of brick, the three-story facility was described as the best-equipped

The second iteration of the Horn and Schwalm Brewery after it had been rebuilt in 1879.

brewery in Wisconsin outside of Milwaukee. It would prove to be just a starting point. It was also the starting point of a new partnership.

Leonhardt Schwalm's son Theodore was now twenty-one and ready to assume the role left open by his deceased father. Schwalm was not even half the age of his partner, August Horn. But the two made a go of it despite the growing realization that Theodore Schwalm was an alcoholic. For now, the problem was manageable. The Brooklyn Brewery surged, pulling ahead of John Glatz at the Union Brewery. In the early 1880s, Horn and Schwalm were selling more beer than any other brewer in Winnebago County.

North of the Fox River, Lorenz Kuenzl at the Gambrinus Brewery was going through his own partnership ordeal. When Kuenzl took over the brewery in 1875, he started with a crew of relatives and holdovers from the Gottlieb Ecke period. Among the relatives was John Walter, the brother of Kuenzl's wife. Walter had been made a partner in the firm in 1876. It didn't work out, and on May 5, 1880, the partnership was dissolved. John Walter left town quietly. That's how it's done when you're leaving with someone else's money.

LOESCHER'S QUANDARY

After being burned out twice, George Loescher thought it would be better to rebuild somewhere else. His new location was about a block west of the old one. The new brewery at the northeast corner of Frankfort Street and Bay Shore Drive was more modern, but its six-hundred-barrel capacity was still tiny in comparison to the five-thousand-barrel capacity of the Glatz brewery a couple miles to his south. Maybe this wasn't such a good idea. Loescher got the new brewery running and then called it quits.

On August 7, 1880, Loescher sold the Oshkosh Brewery to Bernard Ruety and John Walter. Ruety had recently left his job as a brewer at the Knapstein Brewery in New London. John Walter appears to have been the same man who had just parted ways with Lorenz Kuenzl at the Gambrinus Brewery. Walter was up to nothing good.

There was trouble from the very beginning. Ruety and Walter couldn't get along. Each wanted the other man to buy out his stake in the brewery. They had taken a $2,000 loan from Loescher to finance the purchase and a month later were low on cash. They took another loan, this one for $300. John Walter took that money and ran. Before leaving town, Walter went visiting saloons to make collections of money owed on beer sales. Walter absconded with that, too. Ruety was ruined. The brewery reverted back into the hands of George Loescher.

Loescher and his son William continued running the Oshkosh Brewery until 1884, when George Loescher died. He was sixty-five. William attempted to keep the brewery going. It had become the smallest and least productive in Winnebago County, and by 1890, it was closed. William Loescher locked the doors and went to work for Lorenz Kuenzl at the Gambrinus Brewery.

MAROONED ON DOTY ISLAND

The field had narrowed. The carefree days of the vagabond brewer were a thing of the past. Batch sizes increased, and the margin for error decreased. Now there was more at stake. The dominant paradigm insisted upon growth. The trick was to grow faster than the debt incurred to fuel expansion. It was a difficult balance to strike. For George Habermehl, the scales tilted wildly.

Habermehl had taken over the Island Brewery in late 1879. Among his first decisions was to demolish it. The tiny and cramped brewery was not fit for his grandiose plans. By the fall of 1880, construction of the new Island Brewery was underway. Habermehl said he was using the Schlitz Brewery in Milwaukee as his model—grand plans indeed. Habermehl's completed brewery was four stories of brick fronting Nicolet Boulevard. It was forty feet wide, one hundred feet long and seventy feet high. Included was a newly developed and expensive cooling device popular with large breweries in Milwaukee. The set-up still required natural ice, but it was the height of modernity compared to Winnebago County's old beer caves. Habermehl claimed he could produce thirty thousand barrels a year from his new place. That may have been a bit of an exaggeration, but not by much.

Habermehl paid dearly for the improvements. He piled up debt in excess of $30,000 (more than $750,000 today). In the beginning, Habermehl managed to stay out in front of it. Nearly every saloon in Neenah and Menasha carried his beer, and saloons weren't the only outlets. The March 15, 1883 edition of the *Menasha Press* reported that "Almost every wet grocery

The Island Brewery around 1880.

Louis Herziger's grocery, meat market and saloon on North Commercial Street in Neenah. A rare Ed. Fueger Lager Beer sign is posted in front.

house in the two cities deals out lager beer manufactured at the Island Brewery." But the stress points were already showing. Upon purchasing the Island Brewery, Habermehl had taken on a partner in the business, a man known only as R. Mueller. The partnership ended in early 1883 as the financial strain escalated. By the fall of 1883, Habermehl was no longer keeping up on payments to his creditors. On August 7, 1884, the first of a series of lawsuits was filed that would lead to Habermehl losing the brewery. Habermehl toughed it out for another year, but by the end of 1885, he was finished. On January 4, 1886, Habermehl lost the brewery to foreclosure.

The Island Brewery sat idle for much of 1886, until it was purchased on October 1 by Edward Fueger. He was the son of Max Fueger, a partner in the J. Obermann Brewery of Milwaukee. At sixteen, Edward Fueger had quit school and gone to work in his father's brewery. By the time young Fueger reached Menasha, he had been exposed to every aspect of the brewery business from grain to glass.

Fueger immediately attempted to ramp up sales by expanding the brewery's reach. Beer from the Island Brewery was being sent out to Appleton, Chilton, Stevens Point, Waupaca and points farther north. Sales may have been growing, but it wasn't long before Fueger found himself in the same predicament as his predecessor. He couldn't sell enough beer to support the expense of his large brewery. The Island Brewery was proving to be a millstone around the neck of every brewer who attempted to operate it. Fueger remained less than two years before losing the property to foreclosure. In early 1888, the Island Brewery went dark once again.

RACE TO THE FUTURE

Less than two miles west of the Island Brewery, the Ehrgott brothers had taken a more conservative approach. In 1881, the Neenah Brewery celebrated its twenty-fifth anniversary. In all that time, the brewery had been the measure of consistency. There had been just one change in ownership. There had been no aggressive expansions or leveraged forays into outside markets. The brewery consistently pumped out its five hundred barrels or so of beer each year and moved stolidly forward. The formula wasn't exciting, but it worked. Or at least it had.

The brewery was overdue for an upgrade. It would come as the partnership of the two brothers was coming to its end. In 1882, Frank Ehrgott left the brewery. He was now directing the bulk of his time toward his Wisconsin Avenue saloon. Adam Ehrgott assumed full ownership of the brewery. Beginning in 1884, Ehrgott made a series of improvements to the Neenah Brewery that included the construction of a new brew house. For the first time, Ehrgott wasn't living in the same building where he brewed. He also added a more up-to-date icehouse. In conjunction with the construction, Ehrgott changed his approach to brewing.

It had long been the norm in Winnebago County that brewers did their own malting. Most German-trained brewers considered it part of the brewing process. Ehrgott had employed the traditional, floor-malting approach. But now he did away with all that and began purchasing his malt from suppliers who specialized in malting. The change may have had something to do with Ehrgott having to run the brewery on his own. Buying malt was more expensive, but it lightened his workload. The changes were for the better, but the improvements illustrate the predicament small brewers found themselves in. Ehrgott was adding icehouses reliant upon block ice cut from Little Lake Butte des Morts at a time when larger breweries were doing away with natural ice and

The Neenah Brewery after its reconstruction in 1884.

replacing it with mechanical refrigeration. Ehrgott could never have afforded to do that.

Horn and Schwalm's Brooklyn Brewery in Oshkosh was one of those reaping the benefits of the emerging technology. Over the course of the late 1880s and into the 1890s, the Brooklyn Brewery undertook an extensive modernization program. The initiative came on the heels of a bleak period. The drinking problem of the firm's junior partner had developed into full-blown alcoholism. Theodore Schwalm was just twenty-five years old and, as the court decreed, "lost to self control." In January 1883, Schwalm was placed under guardianship due to his excessive drinking. He briefly rebounded, then relapsed. There was no redemption this time. On January 17, 1888, the *Oshkosh Daily Northwestern* reported that Schwalm was gravely ill. Later that day, he died from "an affection of the liver." Theodore Schwalm was twenty-nine years old.

Schwalm's widow, twenty-eight-year-old Sophia Schwalm, became August Horn's new partner. She was Horn's fourth since he'd signed on with Leonhardt Schwalm in 1866. This partnership clicked. It's not known exactly what role Sophia Schwalm played at the brewery, but the change was evident. Horn and Schwalm were looking to the future.

Commercial brewing underwent a series of radical developments in the last quarter of the nineteenth century. The craft of brewing was transformed by advances in biology and technology. No part of the process went untouched. Floor malting, done by hand with shovels and rakes, gave way to machine-driven pneumatic malting. Yeast was no longer the magical, mystifying element it had been. Now it could be isolated and propagated from a single cell, predictable and pure. Direct fire kettles were replaced by steam-heated boilers. For brewers of lager beer, there was perhaps no more pivotal change than the introduction of mechanical refrigeration.

HORN & SCHWALM,

27 to 39 Doty Street.   27 to 39 Doty Street.

BROOKLYN BREWERY.

(SOUTH SIDE)

OSHKOSH,   WISCONSIN.

From Polk's 1884 *Oshkosh City Directory.*

In 1890, Horn and Schwalm became the first brewers in Winnebago County to bring mechanical refrigeration into their brewery. It would put an end to the old habit of cutting tons of ice from Lake Winnebago each winter. It meant precise control over fermentation and aging temperatures. And it allowed the brewery to store hops in a climate that would retain their viability for years instead of months. The ice machine was followed by a new boiler house. A new washing house followed that. It could accommodate a full train carload of kegs. A rail spur was run up to the brewery, over three miles of piping was installed within the plant, and 31 additional lagering vats were added, each of them big enough to hold 140 barrels of beer. By the end of 1891, the Brooklyn Brewery had a 20,000-barrel capacity and was selling beer in every city in the surrounding area. The brewery's lead kept growing.

That kind of expenditure was beyond the means of other Winnebago County brewers, but a lack of capital didn't necessarily cage development. Apart from increased capacity, brewers were growing in other ways. Advances in brewing science were being disseminated widely through trade publications. Any brewer so wanting could avail himself of the information. It was a far cry from the old days.

Gambrinus Brewery.

LORENZ KUENZL, Propr.

OSHKOSH, WISCONSIN.

BREWER AND BOTTLER OF THE CELEBRATED

WEINER, PILSENER, KULMBACHER

AND

SELECT LAGER BEER

FOR HOME TRADE and ALL PARTS of the COUNTRY.

A range of styles produced by the Gambrinus Brewery, from the 1888–89 *Wisconsin State Gazetteer*.

In 1850, when Joseph Schussler was brewing in Oshkosh, he claimed to have a process uniquely his own and known only to himself. For his era, Schussler was a highly skilled brewer. Yet much of what occurred during the process of making beer was mysterious even to him. Schussler knew what worked, but he didn't know why. The limitations of his knowledge limited what he could do in the brew house. And it's why he spoke of his brewing in a way that made it sound like alchemy. In the 1880s, the alchemy was exposed by chemistry.

At the Gambrinus Brewery on Harney Avenue in Oshkosh, Lorenz Kuenzl was one of those brewers doing things in a new way. The Bohemian expat brought his taste for Bohemian lagers with him. To make those beers in Oshkosh, Kuenzl had to manipulate his ingredients in ways his predecessors couldn't.

The early lagers brewed in Winnebago County were deep-amber or brown beers. The color was derived from the darkness of the malt. It was the only style of malt most brewers were able to reliably produce. Kuenzl was able to create a pale malt that led to a lighter-colored beer. Unlike the dark malt, though, Kuenzl's pale malt didn't pair well with the chemical composition of Winnebago County's water. Kuenzl addressed that with a retinue of salts and acids to adjust his brewing liquor. It enabled him to produce a brilliant, golden pilsner with a delicate hop bouquet.

The introduction of adjuncts was another sign of the innovative times. In Winnebago County, adjuncts typically took the form of corn and rice. It's likely that by the late 1870s, the county's brewers had begun dabbling with corn in their beer. By the late 1880s, it was commonplace and for good reason. The locally grown six-row barley came with a high protein content. That was all right for a beer kept cool in a keg, but it spelled trouble for bottled beer that might have to sit on a warm shelf waiting to be purchased. In the bottle, the all-malt beers were inclined to turn hazy and go off. The high protein level of Wisconsin's barley was the culprit. Kuenzl began swapping out a portion of that barley with either corn or rice, both of which he kept on hand. Less barley in the grist meant lower protein levels and a more shelf-stable beer. The sweet spot was a mix of

The Gambrinus Brewery in the early 1890s. Lorenz Kuenzl is seen in white sleeves in front of the brewery's massive stone-and-brick icehouse.

about 25 percent adjunct grain and 75 percent malted barley. As bottled beer grew in popularity, so did the use of corn and rice.

If he'd had his druthers, Kuenzl would probably have preferred to use neither. Both ingredients were more expensive than barley, and they complicated the brewing process. But once Kuenzl had gone down that road, there was no going back. People loved these light-bodied pale beers. By the turn of the century, corn, especially, had become elemental to the beers of Winnebago County.

The Ashes of Menasha

Some brewers embraced the future. Others had it thrust upon them. Werner Winz was going the hard way. Winz had purchased the brewery at First and Manitowoc Streets on December 27, 1880. At that point, the facility was going into its twenty-fifth year. Over the next fifteen years, Winz made a few ancillary upgrades, but the place remained more 1850s than 1890s.

An even more powerful reminder of the past was the partner Winz took on. In January 1881, Winz sold half his interest in the brewery back to Frederick Loescher, who was now sixty years old. For the next eight years, he could call the brewery partly his own again. Loescher retired for good in 1889 after thirty-seven years of involvement with Winnebago County breweries.

Winz couldn't continue drifting along this way if he hoped to stay viable. By the late 1880s, the beer market in Menasha had grown too competitive for such a casual approach. With Loescher's exit, Winz took on a group of investors and incorporated the business as the Menasha Brewing Company. On April 10, 1889, brewery ownership was transferred to the corporation. Werner Winz was named corporation president and general manager. His son Peter became the secretary. Still, things continued to lag.

By 1893, Menasha Brewing was in dire straits. Its home base was flooded with beer. It came not just from Menasha's two breweries but also from breweries in Milwaukee and Oshkosh. Winz had been sending his beer into Appleton and other nearby communities but was being displaced there, as well. The brewery lurched into the red. On August 27, 1894, the property of Menasha Brewing went into foreclosure for nonpayment of taxes. Then came the fire.

At 4:00 a.m. on Sunday, May 19, 1895, the brewery was discovered wrapped in flames. The main section was veneered with brick but constructed

Menasha Brewing after it had been rebuilt in 1895.

of wood. The blaze ripped through it. The destruction of the brew house was total. Even before the last embers were doused, Winz had contacted an architect to request plans for a larger brewery. And he made a point of telling the *Menasha Press* that he had enough beer in his icehouse to continue filling orders through December. Winz couldn't have planned it any better. Just prior to the fire, the brewery had been dark and empty. Papers across the state reported that arson was suspected, but these suspicions were never proven. Whatever the cause, the timing of the fire was extraordinary. The brewery had been on the verge of failure, but three months after the fire, Winz had collected the insurance money and paid off the back taxes. The rest of the windfall went into rebuilding his brewery.

The new facility would put Menasha Brewing on a more competitive footing. The brewery was three stories high and solid brick. It was steam powered, steam heated and lit with lamps. Natural ice was still required for cooling, but most of the cellaring had been brought up from underground into a more efficient icehouse. With its larger capacity and adjacent bottling plant, Menasha Brewing had been rescued from obsolescence. By the late 1890s, the brewery had quadrupled its output to about five thousand barrels annually. Werner Winz was back in the race, another brewer inspired by fire.

THE BROTHERS WALTER

Across the Menasha Channel, nobody had yet managed to figure out what to do with the mammoth Island Brewery. For much of 1888 and 1889, the brewery was idle again. Not that there wasn't interest—in January 1888, the brewery was inspected by John Arensdorf, a brewer from Sioux City, Iowa, looking to make a fresh start. A couple of months earlier, Arensdorf had received a controversial acquittal in the murder of a clergyman who had been agitating for prohibition. To the relief of Menasha's temperance supporters, Arensdorf decided to keep shopping.

On December 18, 1889, the Island Brewery was finally sold out of receivership. At $9,000, it was a steal—the property was valued at more than four times that amount. On the receiving end of the bargain were three deeply experienced brewers, Frank Fries and brothers Christian and Martin Walter. Fries came up in a brewing family. From 1870 until 1885, the Fries family owned what was later renamed George Walter's Star Brewery in Appleton. George Walter was the brother of Christian and Martin. They were part of another great family of brewers. The Walters came from Germany in the early 1870s to spread foam across Wisconsin. George Walter settled in Appleton, where he ran the aforementioned Star Brewery. His brother John Walter went to Eau Claire and established the long-lived John Walter Brewing Company. Christian worked as a journeyman brewer in Appleton, Kenosha, Madison, Milwaukee and Racine before arriving in Menasha. Martin had been brewing since he was fourteen, having learned the trade in several large German breweries. In America, Martin brewed in Appleton, New London and at Schlitz in Milwaukee. If Christian and Martin Walter couldn't make a go of the troubled Island Brewery, nobody could.

The Island Brewery was already an imposing facility. The Walter brothers made it more so. In the run-up to 1900, almost the entire plant was renovated. An enormous malt house was constructed, mechanical refrigeration was installed and a bottling house was built. There had been changes to the law, but it was still illegal to bottle beer within a brewery, so the Walter brothers did the next best thing: they ran a long pipe from the back of the brewery to the bottling house and pushed beer through it with a steam-powered pump. Frank Fries missed most of the excitement. He was gone after a year. Fries went back to Appleton and launched the Appleton Brewing & Malting Company in the building currently occupied by Stone Arch Brewpub. After Fries left, Christian and Martin Walter rechristened their brewery, incorporating it in 1894 as the Walter Brothers Brewing Company.

The Walter brothers had come to town just as the so-called "Beer War" was heating up in Neenah-Menasha. The battle pitted local brewers against "foreign" intruders from Milwaukee. Miller was a primary aggressor, cutting deals with bottlers and saloon operators. The Walter brothers countered by establishing a string of saloons that sold only their beer. They put agents on the streets to sell beer from wagons. Eventually, they gained the upper hand. But the Walters were looking beyond Menasha. The Island Brewery had been sending its beer into northern Wisconsin for years. The Walters liked that strategy. They pushed hard into the territory, using the Wisconsin

Left: From the Semi-Centennial Souvenir Edition of the *Menasha Press*, June 1898.

Right: A pre-Prohibition label for Walter Brothers Porter, a style rarely brewed at the turn of the century in Northeastern Wisconsin.

Central Railway as their conduit. The Walters began selling kegged beer and their bottled Export Beer across much of northern Wisconsin and into the Upper Peninsula of Michigan. In Wisconsin, the brewery built cold-storage warehouses in Custer, Fifield, Ladysmith, Superior and Waupaca. The Walters were doing to small brewers in the north what Milwaukee brewers had tried doing to them.

In 1898, the brothers ventured further afield. Looking to establish a second branch of the brewery, Martin Walter was dispatched on a tour of prospective sites in the West. He settled on Pueblo, Colorado. On July 8, 1898, the Walter brothers acquired the struggling Pueblo Brewery for $7,000. Martin moved west and became the brewery's president and brewmaster. Christian remained in Menasha as president of the Wisconsin plant. Their brother Jacob, who had come to America in 1892, took over Martin's post as vice president in Menasha. The two breweries shared board members but operated as individual entities. Crossover branding lent each business marketing heft. The suggestion, however, of this being a coordinated, cross-country effort was mostly cosmetic. Still, it was a bold move. The audaciousness that epitomized the Walter brothers was paying off. The big brewery on the island was finally realizing its potential.

BREWERS COMBINE

By 1890, more than a half-dozen breweries from outside Winnebago County were vying for the attention of beer drinkers within the county. They came to exploit the notoriously high rates of consumption. The average American drank 13.6 gallons of beer annually. In Winnebago County, they consumed twice that. In Oshkosh, it was even higher: from 28 to 31 gallons per person. Brewers across the nation wanted in. The initial thrust came in the form of beer agents. They lived in the county but were employed by distant breweries to peddle beer to local barmen and retailers. From there it progressed to saloons. By the turn of the century, more than a dozen saloons operating in Winnebago County were under the control of outside breweries. They weren't confined to just Menasha, Neenah and Oshkosh. Butte des Morts, Omro and Winneconne all had saloons connected to distant breweries.

The concentration was greatest in Oshkosh. In 1891, the *Oshkosh Times* reported that "nearly all the large brewing companies of the country have established—or will soon do so—warehouses and branch offices here." Breweries from Cincinnati, Milwaukee and St. Louis were among them. Miller, Pabst and Schlitz built bottling houses in the city. Schlitz owned two downtown saloons. Pabst had at least five saloons in Oshkosh. This was all in addition to the city's own four breweries. People in Oshkosh drank a lot of beer, but they couldn't drink that much.

Battling the outside breweries was tough enough, but the competition from fellow Oshkosh brewers was even worse. Saloon owners played brewers against one another. If Kuenzl was willing to sell his beer for seven dollars a barrel, why not go see if Glatz would sell his for six dollars? More often than not, the tactic worked. Oshkosh's three largest breweries—Glatz's Union Brewery, Horn and Schwalm's Brooklyn Brewery and Kuenzl's Gambrinus Brewery—were caught up in a degenerative pricing battle that threatened to cripple all of them. On May 15, 1893, they agreed to do something about it.

August Horn, John Galtz and Lorenz Kuenzl created a price-fixing scheme. Like most forms of price-fixing in 1893, it was perfectly legal. Its purpose was to protect them from manipulative saloonists. The brewers

Charles Raasch's saloon on North Main Street in Oshkosh. Signs for both the Glatz and Kuenzl breweries are posted at the entrance.

agreed to sell beer at no less than $7.20 a barrel and to limit the amount of money they spent in saloons treating other patrons to rounds of beer. This was no small matter. August Horn, for example, would sometimes visit up to thirty saloons a week, buying rounds of beer in each of them. They also agreed to stop sponsoring "dancing parties" at saloons. This last provision may have been a veiled allusion to picking up the tab for services rendered by prostitutes. In Oshkosh, saloon "dancing parties" and prostitution went hand in glove. The agreement didn't work. Within the year, the scheme was in shambles. Meanwhile, the beer from beyond kept on pouring in. There was only one thing left to do.

On March 21, 1894, Glatz, Horn and Schwalm and Kuenzl merged their breweries to form the Oshkosh Brewing Company. "Through the influx of foreign beer, competition has become so strong that in order to cope with it, these companies have been compelled to combine their interests," the *Oshkosh Times* reported. The paper noted that the merger would "undoubtedly attract considerable attention throughout the state and country." The new brewery, with a capacity of ninety thousand barrels annually, was far and away the largest in the region. August Horn was made company president. John

Glatz became vice president. Lorenz Kuenzl was named superintendent and brewmaster. They had much to work out. High on the list was how to operate three separate facilities in concert without squandering the fiscal advantages gained by the merger. It would take a few years before the Oshkosh Brewing Company would realize its potential. Once it did, there was no stopping it.

For the first time in forty years, Oshkosh was home to just two breweries. The gap separating the two was immense, but over at the Rahr brewery, there were no signs of distress. The Rahr family had been at it now for thirty years. In that time, they had figured out a way to thrive in a market hostile to small brewers. Amid the flux and disruption, the Rahrs carved a singular path.

Charles and Charlie

The Rahr brewery was like none of the others. From the outset, Rahr had been something of an outlier. It was bigger than the county's earlier frontier breweries, but others had surpassed it. And while the others sought growth by building up, boosting capacity and broadening their market, the Rahrs stood pat. The wood-frame brewery Charles and August Rahr built in 1865 hadn't changed much. Production ticked steadily upward, but the numbers remained modest. By the mid-1880s, output hovered around seven hundred barrels annually. That was a good way to get crushed. Breweries this size were being snuffed one after another. But the Rahrs were in no danger. They had something the others didn't: a network of saloons.

They were commonly known as tied houses—places either owned outright by a brewery or under a brewery's financial control. The arrangements varied. The brewery might pay a saloon keeper's licensing fees or foot the bill for heating fuel. Interest-free loans were another way of tying a place up. The Rahrs liked to actually own their tied houses. Whatever the arrangement, the upshot was the same. If you stepped into a tied house, the only beer you'd find there was that of the brewery it was tied to. As a customer, it limited your options. As a brewer, it meant nobody was going to undercut you on pricing. It made for a stable way of doing business. There was nothing new about tied houses. They had been around for as long as there had been breweries. But in Winnebago County, the Rahrs had been unique in building up their network earlier than others. They had begun purchasing saloon properties in Oshkosh by the late 1860s. They were into Butte des

A corner sign for the Rahr Brewery around 1886.

Morts by the 1870s. In all, the Rahrs would tie up approximately twenty saloons. It was the shield defending them from the aggressive ways of much larger breweries.

Their business model was conservative, but the Rahrs never let things get too calm. The partnership between August and Charles Rahr fell apart in 1883. Charles kept the brewery. August went into bottling, running a plant across the street from the brewery where he packaged his brother's beer. Both of them ran into trouble with the law. They had a habit of skirting taxes on the beer they sold. Nothing too serious ever came of it.

The brewery itself continued to be a hangout for the sort of characters Charles Rahr liked to assemble. "In fact, the wildest stories have been set afloat, about secret meetings held nightly by Mr. Weisbrod [Oshkosh undertaker and captain of its fire department] and his friends at Rahr's brewery," the *Daily Northwestern* clucked. The paper of record never looked kindly upon the goings-on at the brewery by the lake. It had been this way for thirty years, and for Charles Rahr, that was enough. Rahr turned sixty in 1896. He wasn't running the brew house anymore. That was being taken care of by his only son, Charles Jr. Nobody called him Junior; everybody called him Charlie.

Charlie Rahr was born in Oshkosh in 1865. He came along just a few months after his father launched the brewery. Charlie grew up there making beer. At fifteen, he quit school and went into the brewery full time. Charlie took correspondence courses in brewing science and spent six months at his cousin's brewery in Manitowoc to see how things were done there. By the time he was twenty-one, Charlie was running the Rahrs' Oshkosh brew house. He wanted to modernize the brewery. Charlie complained that everything was worn out. His father disagreed. Their relationship had never been good, but now it got worse. Charlie said his father treated him more like a servant than a son. Even though he had a wife and two children, Charlie still drew no pay at the brewery. If he needed money, he had to go to Papa with hat in hand. Resentment consumed him. Charlie would never overcome it. He would later say, "He was no father to me. He was my worst enemy." Despite the rancor, Charlie had his way with the brewery.

Charles Rahr Jr., known to all as Charlie.

In 1896, the Rahrs implemented a series of improvements. A new brew house was built, and the old 8-barrel kettle was replaced with a 45-barrel copper. The wooden mash tubs were scrapped, and a new 135-barrel steel cooker was put in. The worn-out equipment that so irritated Charlie was gone. Everything that went in was new. Upon completion of the project, Charles deeded the brewery property to his son. The brewery was renamed

Rahr & Son. Perhaps it was an attempt to make amends, a way to recognize Charlie's contribution. But his father hadn't ceded control. Charles still held the money and the managerial reins. Charlie's sphere of influence was within the brew house. The rest of it remained in the grip of his father.

Charlie made good on the new brew house. Within a year of its completion, output increased almost twofold to two thousand barrels. The quality of that beer was said to be exceptional. As the smallest brewery in the city, the Rahrs would rely on that reputation to sell their beer for decades to come. It wasn't always pretty, but the Rahrs remained strong at a time when breweries such as theirs were succumbing to irrelevance.

At the end of the nineteenth century, the first great transformation of brewing in Winnebago County was complete. All the breweries built before the Civil War had been put out of business, burned down or torn down. The village and neighborhood breweries producing hundreds of barrels each year were gone. They gave way to industrial firms that produced thousands of barrels. The beer was different, too. The dark country lagers made of water, malt, hops and yeast had fallen out of fashion. Both the local palate and local brewers had grown more sophisticated. Corn and rice were introduced to make beer that was delicate, pale and consistent. The beer was becoming more uniform and less an expression of any one brewer's idiosyncratic approach.

The transformation mirrored the changes in Winnebago County. From 1880 to 1900, the county's population tripled. The majority of its sixty thousand residents now lived in cities. More than 65 percent of them were in Menasha, Neenah and Oshkosh. Increasingly, they worked in factories and in professions not directly connected to farming. These people had a different outlook, especially where beer was concerned. Unlike their immigrant forebears, they didn't approach it as a sustaining repast. Beer had become a leisure-time pursuit, a commodity marketed and distributed like any other. These nascent changes would find their full expression in the new millennium.

7

1900-1920

THE CRASHING TIDE

The twentieth century began with five breweries in Winnebago County: one in Neenah, two in Menasha and two in Oshkosh. It had come to this from the peak of the 1870s, when more than a dozen had been in operation. The winnowing wasn't over.

Adam Ehrgott must have felt as if there were a target on his back. He'd been in sole possession of the Neenah Brewery since 1882. Back then, he'd had plans for growing the place. He invested in the business and made improvements to the brewery. But he was always playing catch-up. Walter Brothers in Menasha could produce forty times what Ehrgott could, and Oshkosh Brewing could produce twice as much as Walter Brothers. It was impossible. Adam Ehrgott was done fighting it. On November 11, 1901, Ehrgott sold the Neenah Brewery. The new man was Henry Angermeyer. He was cut from the classic mold.

A German-born brewer, Angermeyer had come to America fifteen years earlier. He was forty-one when he reached Neenah. He'd spent the last few years brewing in Sterling, Illinois. Things were tough there, too. Like the small brewery in Neenah, the small brewery in Sterling was struggling with larger competitors running amuck in the home territory. In Neenah, Angermeyer was going solo. This would be the last brewery in Winnebago County run solely by its owner. It was a stripped-down operation. It had to be. Angermeyer had the only brewery in the county without some form of mechanical refrigeration and the only one without a bottling operation. Angermeyer had gotten what he'd paid for—the

$4,500 sale price wasn't much for a brewery, but in 1901, this wasn't much of a brewery.

Small breweries on the verge of extinction rarely make news unless they go bankrupt or something awful occurs. Angermeyer would have been better off going bankrupt. On the evening of August 4, 1905, he and another man were rowing a skiff loaded with wood across the Neenah Slough. They were near the Main Street bridge, not far from the brewery, when they spotted a floating railroad tie, and Angermeyer tried to pull it aboard. The boat capsized. The other man swam to shore; Angermeyer didn't. They found his body later that night. Henry Angermeyer was pronounced dead at 9:45 p.m. He left a wife and three children. The oldest was a boy of thirteen, too young to take over for his father. Following Angermeyer's death, the brewery remained operational. Just who was running it is unknown. His widow, Lizzie, didn't want to deal with it. She put the brewery up for sale. It took more than a year to find a buyer.

Oscar Doerr purchased the Neenah Brewery on October 19, 1906. He got it for a song, paying just over $3,000. Doerr was coming from Chicago's White Eagle Brewery, where he had been the brewmaster. Doerr had big plans for Neenah. He was going to bring in a bottling line. He told the *Western Brewer*, a trade journal, that he would improve the brewery substantially. Doerr didn't receive an especially warm reception in Neenah. Not long after moving in, his home was robbed by the son of Frank Ehrgott, the former owner of the brewery. Not long after, young Ehrgott got drunk in Oshkosh and fell under a train. His corpse was distributed over hundreds of yards.

Back at the brewery, Doerr had decided the place was too decrepit to make beer in. He made a deal with Werner Winz to have his beer produced by the Menasha Brewing Company. In the meantime, Doerr would attempt to rehabilitate his brewery. The wisdom of contracting your brewing out to a local competitor was debatable. The outcome was not. The Neenah Brewery would not be revived. Doerr officially abandoned the project on January 3, 1910. He sold the facility to Neenah resident Louis Sorenson. The $4,100 sale price would indicate Doerr's planned improvements never materialized. It also appears Doerr had left Neenah well before the sale.

Louis Sorenson made his home at the brewery, but there's no record of him making beer there. Rumors circulated that Walter Brothers wanted it. Christian Walter denied the claims while steadily tightening his grip on Neenah. In 1909, Walter Brothers began construction of a hotel at 210 Main Street that would be the Neenah showcase for the Walter Brothers

After the 1968 fire at what had been the Neenah Brewery. *Courtesy of Douglas Bisel.*

brand. The persistent rumors were confirmed on April 21, 1911, when Walter Brothers purchased the Neenah Brewery. Sorenson moved out, and Christian Walter had the brewery gutted and converted into the Lakeside Hotel and Tavern. It wasn't long before people forgot there had ever been a brewery there.

More than one hundred years earlier, someone asked John Robbins Kimberly where a good place for a brewery might be. "In Hell" was Kimberly's acerbic response. The old Neenah Brewery was destroyed by fire in 1968. Kimberly would have thought it a fitting end.

On a Rising Tide of Beer

The four remaining Winnebago County breweries were in equilibrium. The county was partitioned north and south. Beer from Menasha Brewing or Walter Brothers rarely found its way south into Oshkosh. Beer from Rahr or Oshkosh Brewing was rarely seen in Neenah or Menasha. The incursions from Milwaukee had been substantially beaten back. Walter Brothers controlled the beer market in Menasha and Neenah. Oshkosh Brewing dominated Oshkosh. In each city were people who preferred something else. Those folks kept Rahr and Menasha Brewing in business. The beer of those two breweries saw little circulation outside their hometowns.

Most beer was served from wooden kegs in saloons. Bottled beer accounted for less than 20 percent of overall sales. Beer in Winnebago County meant social drinking in public houses. That put the Oshkosh breweries at an advantage. In 1900, Oshkosh's population of 28,284 had one saloon for every 230 people. Menasha (population 5,589) had one saloon for every 243. Neenah (population 5,954) had one for every 259 of its residents. Increasingly, those saloons were under the influence of the brewery providing the beer they served. By the turn of the century, tied houses were ubiquitous throughout the county. That didn't mean the breweries weren't still going at it. They fought in places like Butte des Morts. Pabst, Rahr, Oshkosh Brewing and Walter Brothers all scuffled there. The intersection of Adams and Main Streets was a battlefield. Rahr came first, establishing a tied house at the northeast corner in 1878. In 1900, Oshkosh Brewing put in a tied house near the southwest corner. In 1902, Pabst took over a saloon at the northwest corner. That same year, Walter Brothers arrived. The brewery would not be outdone. At the southeast corner, Walter Brothers built a stylish saloon and hotel known today as Jimmie's White House Inn.

Both Oshkosh Brewing and Walter Brothers built a number of tied houses that were architecturally significant. The Hotel Menasha was perhaps the best example. In 1905, Christian Walter commissioned Oshkosh architect William Waters to design a showpiece hotel for the corner of Main and Mill Streets in Menasha. It was to be "more conveniently appointed and more elegant in its furnishing than any other in this vicinity." The brewers of Winnebago County had come a long way from the days of dealing their beer from the back door of a brew house.

The houses they lived in were a testament to their success. August Horn, Christian Walter and John Glatz all built grand homes for themselves. The Glatz family home included a subtle flair reflecting the pugnacity of its main

Left: An etched Walter Brothers glass from the early 1900s. Such glasses were often used in tied-house saloons.

Below: The former home of John Glatz in Oshkosh. *Courtesy of Mike Douglas.*

occupant. Along the roofline were broken beer bottles embedded in plaster. The shards were supposedly from the bottles of former rivals, like a crown made from the remains of vanquished opponents. Obviously, Glatz was still in touch with the elemental urges that drove him halfway around the world forty years earlier.

All the fineries were paid for by beer. That too had acquired a new level of sophistication. Foaming dark lager was now just one option among many. Oshkosh Brewing offered upwards of seven different beers at any given time.

The continually expanding Walter Brothers Brewery, from *Illustrated Menasha*, 1913.

Among them were a light-bodied weiss beer, an amber Vienna-style lager and a delicate pilsner made with rice and imported hops. Walter Brothers also had a weiss beer in its list. Further down was a dark porter, a style not often seen in northeast Wisconsin. Menasha Brewing produced several brands, including its Export Beer. The pale, bitter and slightly stronger lager was made to capture the attention of a more refined palate. After building their new bottling plant in 1915, the Rahrs introduced a light-amber and malty lager named Elk's Head. It became Rahr's flagship brand. Some later claimed it was the best beer ever produced in Oshkosh.

These were heady times for the breweries that had managed to survive. Production figures from the period are somewhat unreliable, but a conservative estimate would put Winnebago County's early-1900s output in the neighborhood of thirty-five thousand barrels annually. It would continue to increase, but it was never enough. The advantage had been gained. Now came the time to exploit it.

THE BIG BREWERY IN OSHKOSH

No other Winnebago County brewery has ever dominated its local market to the degree Oshkosh Brewing did in the early 1900s. It was the largest brewery in the county in the county's largest city. If you were going to sell beer in Oshkosh, you were going to do it on the Oshkosh Brewing Company's terms.

The beginning hadn't looked so promising. The first year was spent trying to get a handle on the operation. Oshkosh Brewing was composed of three separate facilities. It was an awkward arrangement. Initially, the Kuenzl brewery was going to be used to make weiss beer. Instead, the brew house was shut down and converted into a bottling plant. Both the Glatz and Horn and Schwalm breweries continued their brewing operations, presumably each producing different beers to maintain a level of consistency. The heads of the three merged breweries had been in competition with one another for nearly twenty years. Now they had to work together. They weren't allowed much time to figure that out. On April 15, 1895, brewery vice president John Glatz died. Brewmaster Lorenz Kuenzl passed away two years later. This wasn't the first time August Horn dealt with this kind of thing. But Horn had never dealt with someone like William Glatz.

William Glatz replaced his father as Oshkosh Brewing's vice president. Glatz was born in 1862 in Milwaukee. He learned the brewing trade from the ground up. His entire life had been spent in and around breweries. The education hadn't ended there. Unlike most young men who came of age in breweries in the 1870s, Glatz went on to high school and college. In 1888, his father made him a full partner in the family brewery. That same year, Glatz married Emma Klann, whose father ran the Cream City Brewing Company in Milwaukee.

Glatz viewed the business of brewing in a manner alien to his foreign-born elders. He continually chided others at the brewery to approach the business in a more "business-like way." August Horn took the brunt of Glatz's

William Glatz.

nagging. Horn was a soft touch. Saloon keepers loved him. He liked to throw money around buying beers for everyone at the bar. He often extended credit to delinquent saloon keepers. By 1896, the past due accounts were running into the tens of thousands. Horn's largest drove William Glatz mad. "Collecting should be pushed more," Glatz wrote in a terse letter to Horn in 1896. "All customers who do not pay should be stopped or made to pay cash."

Horn would never change, but by 1900, William Glatz's influence was becoming apparent. The early lack of direction gave way to a sense of purpose that drove the brewery forward. Glatz was all about the bottom line. For saloon keepers, that meant pay up or get cut off and dragged into court. They threatened to revolt and buy their beer from other breweries. Glatz knew they wouldn't. When people walked into an Oshkosh saloon they expected to find Oshkosh Brewing's beer there. The city had more than one hundred saloons. Aside from tied houses owned by other breweries, every one of them carried Oshkosh. The beer had become synonymous with the city.

Oshkosh Brewing played the hometown mantra to the hilt. Newspaper advertisements suggested that drinking Oshkosh Beer was a civic duty. "The company prefers home-grown cereals. Every bushel is bought in Oshkosh in open market at the highest prices. It assures the farmer of better prices for his grain, and thus indirectly rebounds to the benefit of the city at large." If hometown pride didn't move you, there was this: "Some of the big outside brewers employ expert chemists to provide substitutes for high priced materials and to find ways of artificially aging beer." Such aspersions were bound to find an audience in an era when food purity had become a primary concern.

By 1903, Oshkosh Brewing was producing 75 percent of all the beer consumed in Oshkosh. Annual production had reached twenty thousand barrels. When August Horn died in 1904, the mantle was passed to William

A postcard from 1915 featuring the Oshkosh Brewing Company.

Glatz. The forty-two-year-old brewery president exerted his whip hand. Oshkosh Brewing was on a spree, buying tied houses and building new saloons. By 1910, the brewery had total control over the Oshkosh beer market. The time had come to build a monument to that success.

In the spring of 1911, construction of a new brewery began next door to the former Horn and Schwalm plant. Glatz hired noted Chicago architect Richard Griesser for the design. Griesser outdid himself. The redbrick brewery covered a good part of the block. It was composed of three asymmetrical sections, the largest being six stories high with a crow-stepped gable roof. The structure loomed over Doty Street. The interior was every bit as impressive. The new brew house could produce 250 barrels of beer at a turn with an annual capacity of 90,000 barrels. This was without question the most advanced brewery in the region.

The new facility was up and running in early May 1912. They wanted to show it off. Oshkosh Brewing held a month-long open house with full tours every Saturday. No doubt they were proud of the place. But there was a shadow cast over the celebration. Its source was the new brewery going up just across the street.

The Peoples Revolt

The Oshkosh Brewing company, controlling all the breweries in this city, has decided on an increase of $1 a barrel in the price of beer to dealers.
—Oshkosh Daily Northwestern, *June 11, 1898*

And that's when things began going to hell. Prior to the 1894 formation of Oshkosh Brewing, the city's saloon keepers had been having their own way. They played the breweries against each other to drive down prices. Now the tables were turned. Oshkosh Brewing dictated prices. If William Glatz decided saloon keepers should pay more for beer, saloon keepers paid more for beer, it was that simple. The saloon keepers hated it. They planned their retaliation. Following the 1898 price hike, a group of about forty local saloonists decided they'd get out from under the yoke of Oshkosh Brewing. Their thought was to revive the old Loescher brewery. They'd hire a brewmaster and make their own beer. It never came to pass, but the idea would not die. It bubbled up every time Oshkosh Brewing put the squeeze on.

The discontent galvanized when Glatz and company began building their new, showpiece brewery. The same week that saw the start of its construction, a group of Oshkosh saloon and business owners met downtown at the Revere Hotel. The leader of the opposition was longtime saloon keeper Joseph Nigl. For almost thirty years, he and his father before him had been running the saloon at the northwest corner of Ninth and Ohio Streets. Nigl had been doing business with Oshkosh Brewing since the brewery's 1894 inception, but the relationship soured in 1897 after the brewery built its own saloon directly across the street from Nigl's place. Nigl commiserated with others who had similar stories of perceived betrayal. Again, the idea of having their own brewery popped up. This time, they decided on a different approach. They'd meet with Charlie Rahr to see if he'd be willing to sell his brewery.

Charlie Rahr was now sole owner of the brewery his father and uncle had launched in 1865. Over the last few years, he'd updated the place thoroughly, even outfitting it with mechanical refrigeration. Rahr had more improvements in the offing. But when the saloon keepers approached him, they found Rahr surprisingly amenable. They came to terms on all but one issue. Rahr wanted them to take not only the brewery but all of the brewery's saloons as well. The last thing the saloon keepers wanted was more saloons. The contingency scotched the deal. A week later, a new plan came forward.

They were now calling their group the Peoples Brewing Company of Oshkosh. Joseph Nigl was its president. On January 12, 1912, Peoples announced it would construct a brewery on the south side of Oshkosh. It would be across the street from the new brewery being built by Oshkosh Brewing. Joseph Nigl was giving William Glatz a dose of his own medicine. Nigl decided to let someone else make the big announcement. The honor went to William Kargus, a former employee of Oshkosh Brewing. Kargus had been fired after a dispute with William Glatz. Now Kargus was working for Peoples. In his statement, Kargus said the new brewery would be a cooperative effort with all sharing in its success. It was another shot at the old boss.

The idea was to have a brewery with diversified ownership spread widely among local residents. In keeping with the brewery's name, the stockholders represented all walks of life. Oshkosh's saloon keepers were well represented, but stock ownership was restricted to prevent any group or individual from taking a controlling interest. Peoples became one of more than fifty cooperative breweries then in operation in the United States.

Brewery construction began on March 26, 1912. Just across the street, Oshkosh Brewing was preparing for the grand opening of its new brewery.

The introduction of Peoples Brewing, *Oshkosh Daily Northwestern*, June 21, 1913.

The state of affairs had William Glatz in an ugly mood. In May, Oshkosh Brewing published a screed in the *Daily Northwestern* denouncing Peoples and maligning its product. Glatz was getting ahead of himself. Peoples had yet to produce a single drop of beer. One can imagine the amusement Nigl and Kargus derived from the conniption of their former overlord.

On June 21, 1913, the Peoples Brewing Company of Oshkosh announced it was open for business. The new, four-story brewery was state of the art. It used electric power and had a twenty-five-thousand-barrel brew house, mechanical refrigeration and a bottling line. No Winnebago County brewery had ever started with such advantages. Better yet, a dedicated customer base was established even before the first barrel rolled out the door. Immediately upon opening, Peoples beer went on tap in more than twenty-five Oshkosh saloons. Many of those places had been Oshkosh Brewing's customers. Not anymore.

For years, a sign for Oshkosh Beer had hung outside the entrance to Joseph Nigl's saloon. It was taken down and replaced by a sign for Peoples

Beer. That was happening all over town. Peoples was an unmitigated success from day one. The grip that Oshkosh Brewing had held on the city's beer market for almost twenty years was broken. If William Glatz thought this was bad, he had another think coming. The worst was yet to come.

FROM OUT OF NOWHERE

Charles Rahr, founder of the Rahr Brewing Company of Oshkosh, was troubled by the way his son Charlie was behaving. It was 1913 and it was Charlie's brewery now, but his father was concerned about the debt Charlie was piling up to modernize the facility. Rahr urged his son to slow down. He warned that Prohibition was coming. Charlie wasn't hearing it. His father died on November 30, 1913. A few months later, Charlie began construction of a new bottling plant.

Before his death, Charles Rahr was one of the few people in Oshkosh who realized what was occurring. The winds had shifted. The incipient scheme to prohibit the production and sale of alcohol in the United States had developed into a looming threat. The Oshkosh brewers paid no mind. They built up and pumped out more beer than ever before. In 1914, the city's three breweries produced fifty thousand barrels of beer. There was no stopping them.

In Menasha, a more sober view prevailed. Perhaps it was the influence of its twin city. Neenah's anti-liquor crusaders were having a field day. Through the city's government, they harassed saloon keepers and brewers alike by enacting punitive licensing requirements. On July 1, 1917, Neenah became the only incorporated city in Winnebago County to vote itself dry. The measure passed by a single vote. Neenah wasn't alone. The town of Oshkosh and the villages of Omro and Winneconne also enacted dry

The look of Rahr's Beer in 1913, when it was being bottled at the Neumueller Brothers plant across the street from the brewery.

laws. In the city of Oshkosh, where no amount of beer was ever too much, it was easy to ignore such things. In Menasha, it was not. In 1909, both Menasha Brewing and Walter Brothers built facilities for the production of soft drinks. They were preparing for what was beginning to look inevitable.

For Walter Brothers, the noose was tightened notch by notch. The bulk of the brewery's sales outside of Neenah and Menasha were in rural areas in northern Wisconsin and the Upper Peninsula of Michigan. Those markets were evaporating. In 1916, Michigan voted itself dry. In northern Wisconsin, Ladysmith, Superior and Waupaca each enacted some form of dry law. Walter Brothers had established distribution facilities in all these places. Now it couldn't sell beer from any of them.

By the summer of 1919, it had finally dawned on brewers in Oshkosh that the threat was real. But the naivete was still intact. Oshkosh Brewing rushed out a nonalcoholic drink named Pep. The first ads for the beverage claimed that it "Solved the Problem" of Prohibition—hardly. One Oshkosh drinker remembered Pep as "A kind of near beer with a lousy taste. Nobody drank that stuff. Everybody wanted something with a wallop." For the breweries, the wallop came in another form. In 1920, national Prohibition arrived. The unthinkable had happened. The breweries of Winnebago County were forbidden by law to make beer.

8

1920-1933

FERAL BEER

There were people who honestly believed that making liquor illegal would make it go away. These people did not live in Winnebago County. On January 17, 1920, the Eighteenth Amendment of the U.S. Constitution went into effect, prohibiting the manufacture, sale or transportation of alcoholic beverages. But even before Prohibition arrived, there was already ample evidence that nothing so temporal as a law would ever make Winnebago County go dry. The Wartime Prohibition Act was instituted six months prior to the start of national Prohibition. The act's intent was identical to that of the Eighteenth Amendment. People in Winnebago County responded with an outburst of home-based liquor distillation and beer making. An underground economy built on moonshine and bootleg beer was immediately established. Those who cared to drink went right on drinking.

Winnebago County's breweries lurched into Prohibition armed with little more than vague plans to outlast the unpopular law. Menasha Brewing would try to survive on its soda business. Rahr Brewing in Oshkosh did the same. Peoples and Walter Brothers would produce near beer in addition to soda. Oshkosh Brewing would do all of that and more, including making malt extract for the suddenly popular hobby of homebrewing. All of them struggled.

Menasha Brewing went dark shortly after the arrival of national Prohibition. Walter Brothers held on, but its ironically named near beer, Dry Cure, was no remedy. In 1922, the brewery's bottling plant was converted

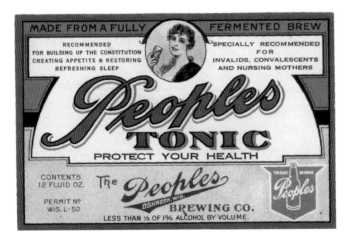

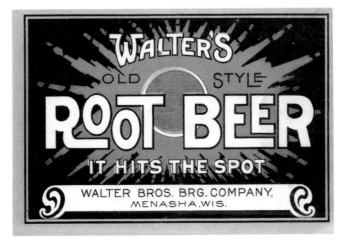

Top: Cans of malt syrup produced by Oshkosh Brewing during Prohibition for the use of homebrewers.

Middle: A Prohibition-era bottle label for nonalcoholic Peoples Tonic.

Bottom: A bottle label for Walter Brothers Root Beer, a popular Menasha repast during Prohibition.

into a knitting factory. Walter Brothers limped along, but its meager existence grew more uncertain each passing year. Oshkosh's three breweries fared slightly better but just barely. They shed workers as their threadbare operations diminished. They became bystanders to an outlaw drinking culture that made do without them.

Winnebago County became notorious for its defiance of the dry law. Roadhouses serving alcohol were in every corner of the county. Federal agents denounced the local sheriff for his lack of support. In Oshkosh, the feds got even less help. "Police in Oshkosh are active and efficient with respect to all law violations, except, of course, those connected with the liquor traffic," one federal agent complained. Oshkosh was home to more than 120 speakeasies. Menasha was accused of having 25. "Neenah is dry and good, while Menasha is wet and bad," federal investigator Frank Buckley observed simplistically in 1931. "Menasha is very wet; it houses a rough foreign element that creates a liquor, prostitution and gambling market. Neenah, on the other hand, leans the other way and tolerates none of the latter vices." Buckley had overlooked Neenah's half-dozen speakeasies, not to mention the bootleg beer brewery run by brothers Albert and Guy Pitt on East Wisconsin Avenue.

They came to be known as "wildcat" breweries. They were as feral as the name implied. They lurked in the basements of forgotten saloons, on side streets in private homes and on farms in nearly every township. Among the great ironies of Prohibition in Winnebago County was the deluge of brewery openings. When beer was still legal, five breweries operated within the county. During the dry years, approximately twenty were at work. The bootleg baron of suds was an Oshkosh roofer turned brewer named Frank "Butch" Youngwirth.

Youngwirth was born in Oshkosh in 1892. He was the son of a Bohemian immigrant couple, the firstborn of their seventeen children. Youngwirth was raised on the south side in the old "bloody" Sixth Ward, where the ambit of social life ranged from church to corner saloon. The secular end of that spectrum was criminalized by the dry law. What had been commonplace took on an illicit allure, just the thing for the freewheeling Youngwirth. He was twenty-nine with a wife and five children when he ditched his day job in 1921 to open a speakeasy on the corner of Sixth and Ohio Streets in Oshkosh. A year later, he was arrested for selling moonshine. He paid the fine and went back to work. They'd never catch him again. Youngwirth got into beer and got ambitious. Accounts vary, but men who worked for him say Youngwirth kept up to seven wildcat breweries in operation.

A rare photograph taken inside an Oshkosh speakeasy in the mid-1920s. Frank "Butch" Youngwirth stands behind the bar. *Courtesy of Wayne Youngwirth.*

"He had quite a few places in town where he could be back in business in 24 hours if the feds came in and busted things up," said a former bootlegger employed by Youngwirth. "He only had one going at a time, but the others were always ready. There was one on Sixth Street, one on Oregon Street; they were all over. He'd pay the guy who owned the land to keep the brewery there, and also to take the rap if they got caught. If the guy got sent to the House of Correction in Milwaukee, Butch would pay him well for the time he spent there."

These were more than tricked-out home breweries. They produced beer on a scale commensurate with contemporary craft breweries. When a Youngwirth wildcat near the corner of Oregon and Fourteenth Streets in Oshkosh was raided, federal agents found a fully equipped production and packaging facility with a four-head bottling line and more than 160 barrels of beer ready for distribution.

Making it illegal caused the price of beer to skyrocket. Just before Prohibition, breweries in Winnebago County were selling beer for about $7.50 a barrel. Near the end of Prohibition, a keg of wildcat beer was selling for $27.50. Youngwirth made a fortune. In one of his better years, he earned

$40,000 on bootleg beer. That would amount to more than $600,000 today. Youngwirth spent all of it. "I remember him and his buddies driving around in their Buicks every Monday to make their collections at the saloons," a Youngwirth associate said. "He was quite a guy. The finest. He was always out and about drinking and gambling. Geez, he was a wildman. Big. About 6-3 and 250 pounds. Everybody knew him," including the people who used to make and sell beer when it was legal.

To keep up with demand, Youngwirth purchased wort from local breweries that his brewers would ferment into beer. Walter Brothers and all three Oshkosh breweries had permits for the production of near beer, so the production of wort within their facilities was legal. What Youngwirth did with it was his business. The folks at the breweries certainly knew what he was up to. And while they floundered, they watched Youngwirth prosper. It's no wonder some went rogue.

Walter Brothers was the first to stray outside the law. On Saturday, July 24, 1920, federal agents visited Menasha to sample Walter Brothers' near beer. As they suspected, it was nearer to real beer than it ought to be. The brewery was hit with an $1,100 fine. After it was discovered that four hundred barrels of the beer had been brewed, penalties were increased to nearly $6,000. The brewery persisted, and in January 1923, Walter Brothers officials were charged with thirteen counts of selling beer and two counts of manufacturing beer. Another stiff fine was passed down. That was the end of Walter Brothers making beer during Prohibition—or at least getting caught doing it.

For the Winz family of the Menasha Brewing Company, the time had arrived for desperate measures. By 1924, the brewery Werner Winz had built up over the past forty years was slipping away. The company was bankrupt. Its property went into receivership. There it languished for three years. Nobody wanted a brewery that couldn't make beer. Meanwhile, Peter Winz, son of Werner, was working to raise funds to get the brewery out of hock. On January 4, 1927, he met his goal and brought the brewery back into the family fold. That wasn't his endgame. By January 1930, it was obvious something was up. The Winz family began playing shell games with the title to the property. Peter Winz, his daughter Helen Schreiter and her husband, Herman Schreiter, shuffled ownership through a convoluted series of transactions. The culmination was a lease to two Milwaukee men named Harry Harris and William Desmond. The lease agreement is an interesting document. It spells out that the brewery was to be used for the production of wort, "a legal brewing product." The brewery was not to be used in any way that may "violate any of the terms of the 18th Amendment or any Prohibition law of the United States." On May 16, 1930, Harris and Desmond took possession. The brewery exploded forty days later.

On the morning of Thursday, June 26, 1930, two 500-gallon vats of alcohol within the brewery burst into flame. The interior of the building caught fire. The blaze raged for more than an hour before Menasha's fire department managed to get it under control. Prohibition agents arrived shortly after. They found one of the largest alcohol distilling plants yet seen in Wisconsin with a capacity of 1,500 gallons a day. They also found nearly 10 tons of sugar in burlap bags and 750 pounds of distiller's yeast. What they didn't find were the people running the place. Peter Winz and company claimed ignorance. Herman Schreiter brushed it off, telling reporters the brewery had been sold two weeks ago to men from Milwaukee. Prohibition agents said that until they could determine the actual owners, no charges would be made. They'd have their work cut out for them. While they untangled the paper trail, a wrecking crew was called up from Fond du Lac to destroy what the fire left behind. It took agents almost a year to figure out what the Winz family was up to. In April 1931, Herman Schreiter and Sylvester Winz, the son of Peter Winz, were arrested and charged with manufacturing liquor. They would all eventually plead guilty. By that time, they were into their next adventure.

On Wednesday, August 5, 1931, the padlocked brewery was raided again. This time, federal agents found beer. The brewery itself was too heavily damaged to have produced it. Instead, it was being used as a storehouse for distribution purposes. Sylvester Winz was arrested again. A month later, his brother Arthur Winz was hauled in. This was a family affair. They all went down together. Over the course of the next year, federal agents built their case against the Winz family. They used the same tactic employed against Al Capone. In December 1932, a year after Capone's conviction, Herman Schreiter, along with Peter, Arthur and Sylvester Winz, pled guilty to tax evasion on income derived from bootlegging. Unlike Capone, they didn't get jail time. For the Winz family, it was stiff fines and a sort of exile. They would never again operate a brewery in Menasha.

While the Winz family was getting punished, other brewers in the county were getting ready for a future that finally looked promising. The death knell for Prohibition was the sweeping victory of the Democrats and President Franklin D. Roosevelt in the November 1932 election. The change came suddenly.

On March 22, 1933, President Roosevelt signed the Beer and Wine Revenue Act. The new law declared beer less than 3.2 percent alcohol by weight (4 percent by volume) to be nonintoxicating and thereby not subject to Prohibition enforcement laws. In Oshkosh, the news reached the breweries by telegraph. They let their whistles blare in a long roar of relief. They already had beer in production. "We're not saying how much we've got, but we've got all we can legally have stored," said a representative of Rahr Brewing. On April 7, 1933, the beer began flowing. On December 5, 1933, the Eighteenth Amendment was repealed. Prohibition was over. Full-strength beer was back. Happy days were here again.

9

1933-1960

THE RETURN OF AN OLD FRIEND

On March 22, 1933, the Oshkosh Brewing Company ran an unintentionally bittersweet ad in the *Daily Northwestern*. It began, "After 14 Years an Old Friend Comes Back." The old friend was indeed coming back, but it was much changed. The disastrous ordeal of Prohibition forever altered America's beer culture and not for the better. The most tangible outcome was the loss of breweries. In 1915, the United States had 1,345 breweries. After Prohibition, that number was reduced to just 766. The count would continue falling. In Winnebago County, though, the picture was somewhat rosier.

In the run-up to repeal, all five of the county's 1919 breweries pledged to resume brewing operations. But it was not going to be as it had been. The five men who had presided over those five breweries died during the dry years. Joseph Nigl of Peoples passed in 1921; Charlie Rahr in 1925; William Glatz of Oshkosh Brewing in 1928; Werner Winz of Menasha Brewing in 1931; and Christian Walter in 1932. The wealth of experience those men possessed went with them. A new era had arrived, and a new generation of brewers would have to figure out how to navigate it. In Oshkosh, the city's three breweries immediately bounced back. The response was overwhelming. "There has been such a heavy demand that it is doubtful whether it will be possible to make all the deliveries that have been promised," reported the *Daily Northwestern*. In Menasha, the demand for beer was just as great. The city's two breweries, however, were in no position to meet it. Walter Brothers was caught off guard. The brewery was in disrepair, and the recent death of

Christian Walter had left the company temporarily rudderless. Things were even worse at Menasha Brewing.

Peter Winz told the press he'd soon have his brewery up and running. What could he have been thinking? Winz was under federal indictment for tax evasion on money made from bootlegging. He had no chance of getting a brewer's permit. Not only that, the brewery—now in his daughter Helen's name—had been damaged by fire and ransacked by federal agents. It was in no way capable of producing beer in the volume required to make a go of things. Whether he accepted it or not, Peter Winz was out of the beer business. His sons Arthur and Sylvester would carry on the family tradition but not at the family brewery. They headed over to Doty Island and went to work at Walter Brothers. It took a couple more years for the Winz family to let go. In 1935, they relinquished the brewery that had been theirs for more than fifty years. The new owners gave it a new name. The purchase would turn out to be far more trouble than it was worth. The road to that realization was a long one.

FOX VALLEY BREWING COMPANY

Even the name turned into a problem. At first, it was going to be Valley Brewing Company. That didn't sit well with a group in Green Bay trying to revive the old Hagemeister Brewery under the same title. So that name was dropped, and in July 1936, Fox Valley Brewing Company was born. In the time it took to resolve that, another set of issues cropped up. The first officers of the endeavor were Joseph Thiel, a Hilbert investor who would act as president; Conrad Rossmeier, a retired farmer from Sherwood who would be vice president; and J.C. Kleesges from Menasha, who was to be the company secretary. The roster fell apart in the summer of 1936 after Thiel sued Kleesges for embezzling $116.18 from company funds. The case was dismissed, and so was Kleesges. He was replaced as secretary by John A. Feiner, a brewer from Milwaukee. Feiner was now living in Menasha and would be the person most responsible for making Fox Valley Brewing a reality.

In the post-Prohibition era, there weren't a lot of young brewers with a lineage like Feiner's around. He was born in 1907 in Winnebago County, Illinois, where his father was brewmaster for Rockford Brewing Company. Shortly after his son's birth, Frank Feiner moved his family to Berlin,

Wisconsin, and became brewmaster and manager of the brewery there. When Prohibition ended, John Feiner began his career in beer working for breweries in Milwaukee and Watertown. Feiner's first job in Menasha was to get the brewery in working order. In August 1936, Fox Valley announced it would be in operation by January 1937. That was wishful thinking. They had yet to even obtain licensing. Almost seventeen years had passed since the facility had last operated as a legitimate brewery. It was in a pitiful state. Feiner must have wondered what he had gotten into when he saw the brewery's towering iron smokestack buckle and then collapse during a storm. He had years of work ahead of him.

Renovation of the brewery proceeded into 1939 with still no beer to show for it. Money grew tight. Contractors weren't getting paid. Neither were the property taxes. In November 1939, Feiner went before the Menasha City Council to plead his case. The brewery was $2,300 in arrears on taxes and facing foreclosure. Feiner explained that he was close to opening the brewery, but that he didn't have enough cash to pay the taxes. He came up with about half of what was owed and cut a deal exempting the brewery from city taxes for the next three years. In exchange, Feiner promised to employ Menasha labor and have Fox Valley up and running within three months. He didn't make it, but he didn't miss by much. By January 1940, the brewery was near completion, but it had again exhausted its working capital. And again there were problems with contractors not being paid. Rossmeier poured in an additional $6,600 to get them over the last hurdle. Finally, there was daylight.

On April 11, 1940, John Feiner brewed the first batch of beer for Fox Valley Brewing Company. The *Menasha Record* reported that the brewery was now "modern in every detail." The old, battered equipment from the Winz days was gone and replaced with new. Feiner said that when the brewery got up to speed, it would employ about a dozen men. In the meantime, Fox Valley needed a name for its beer. Feiner said he was looking for suggestions. He missed an opportunity to play on regional pride and bypassed labeling it Fox Valley Beer. His own pride may have gotten in the way. In the end, it was named Feiner Beer.

By the early summer of 1940, Fox Valley's keg beer was being sold in taverns. Menasha and Neenah were the main markets, but the brewery also distributed into Appleton and Oshkosh. Drinkers were not especially impressed. The problem may not have been the beer but the package. During its first six months of operation, Fox Valley offered only kegged beer. Most taverns had three or fewer draft lines. Each of those lines was usually

Tap knobs issued by Fox Valley Brewing in the early 1940s.

dedicated to a particular beer or brewery. A new brewery trying to wedge its way in faced an uphill battle.

In September 1940, Fox Valley purchased bottling equipment. A month later, Feiner Beer in bottles began making the rounds. It helped but not enough. Reports from 1941 show the brewery producing less than two thousand barrels for the year. In comparison, Walter Brothers was producing more than six times that amount. Perhaps more troubling was the lack of enthusiasm for Feiner Beer in bottles. In an era when sales of bottled beer were beginning to surpass that of kegged beer, bottled beer remained a fraction of Fox Valley's overall output.

By the fall of 1941, Fox Valley was already in trouble. Walter Brothers, dominant in the market, consistently undercut Fox Valley on price. With little money in reserve for advertising, the brewery had difficulty attracting a following. By the end of 1941, the business was coming undone. One of the last notices for the brewery came in January 1942, when Feiner placed an advertisement in the *Menasha Record* congratulating George Sahotsky upon the opening of his Club Tavern, where Feiner Beer would be served. By that time, both Thiel and Rossmeier had left the fold. John Feiner was now president and brewmaster and occupying just about every other role at the brewery.

Fox Valley teetered into the first quarter of 1942. In quarter two, it collapsed. On April 17, Fox Valley's creditors petitioned for the brewery's

The November 19, 1940 announcement that Feiner Beer would finally be available in bottles.

involuntary bankruptcy. On May 4, the brewery was adjudicated bankrupt and closed by the court. The property reverted to Conrad Rossmeier and was later acquired by the City of Menasha. In 1856, Orville Hall and Frederick Loescher began moving Menasha's first brewery across town to its new site at 101 Manitowoc Street. In 1987, the vacant brewery there was demolished to make way for what is now Winz Park.

A FAMILY BREWERY

And then there were four. Only one of them was still family-owned. The Rahr family had grown their brewery slowly and steadily. Their approach had always been conservative. Now the third generation of Rahr family members was in control. The continuity was at odds with the discontinuity of the post-Prohibition period. The challenge of the new era fell to a young trio.

A label for Elk's Head Beer from the early 1930s.

In 1917, Charlie Rahr transferred ownership of the brewery to his three children, Blanche, Carl and Lucille. At twenty-four, Blanche was the oldest, but the three of them were experienced beyond their years. They had grown up at the brewery. Running it was part of their everyday life. Besides, they always had their father to go to if there were questions. Then came Prohibition, which nobody had an answer to. And in the midst of that came the death of their father in 1925. When Prohibition ended, the store of familial knowledge the Rahrs had accrued counted for less than it ever had. What was there to do but follow the tradition? The Rahrs picked up where the Rahrs left off.

They brought back Elk's Head, the brewery's pre-Prohibition lager. In the decade leading to Prohibition, the trend toward lighter, paler beers was already strongly in evidence. Elk's Head resisted the drift. It remained more robust than its better-known competitors. The reason for the resistance to change may have had something to do with the places where the beer was consumed. Before Prohibition, much of Rahr's beer was poured in the brewery's tied-house saloons, where the only beer on the bar was the amber-hued Elk's Head. There was nothing like Schlitz Extra-Pale on hand to compare it to. The controlled environment made the Rahrs less vulnerable to the shift, driven by larger breweries, toward a more neutral, less flavorful product.

When Prohibition ended, Elk's Head came back fully intact. The beer was heavily promoted. The first notices were an appeal to those seeking the "old-fashioned beer that old-timers remember." Elk's Head was "full-bodied" with a "velvety smoothness" and a "heavy richness." In a world given over to increasingly mild beer, Elk's Head stood out and not necessarily in a good way. The tied-house system was gone, and now Elk's Head was sharing

Blanche Rahr.

the bar with the latest iteration of lighter lagers. The Rahrs' beer may have struck a chord with the old-timers, but for the new generation of drinkers, Elk's Head was as claimed: strictly old-fashioned. The people behind that beer were anything but.

Brother and sister Carl and Blanche Rahr took the lead at the brewery. Carl was thirty-eight when Prohibition ended. Blanche was forty-one. Carl was brewmaster and oversaw the day-to-day operations of getting the beer out. Blanche was involved in most everything else. She'd been working at the brewery since she was fourteen. She became its treasurer when she turned eighteen. Blanche Rahr wasn't the first woman to play a prominent role in a Winnebago County brewery, but she was the first whose prominence was made explicit. In many ways, Blanche was the public face of the brewery. Known for speaking her mind, she was the one reporters went to when they needed a quote. She had famous friends in California, and updates from her busy social life made their way into the *Daily Northwestern*. Despite her modern manner, the tradition she came from remained important.

Blanche promoted the fact that this was a legacy brewery bonded to family history. "Several lifetimes in the Rahr family have been devoted to the brewing of fine beer. We are proud of our beer and justly so!", was a quote featured in advertising for the brewery in the late 1930s. Elk's Head had a reputation for quality, but its audience was dwindling. Rahr beer was confined to Winnebago County. Oshkosh was where most of it was poured along with limited distribution in Butte des Morts, Omro and Winneconne. But in all those places, it was being bottom-shelfed by tavern owners wooed by breweries providing incentives that dwarfed anything the Rahrs could offer.

By 1940, production had fallen below the ten to twelve thousand barrels the brewery had annually produced some twenty years earlier. Yet the Rahrs managed to endure, as did Elk's Head. Charles Rahr III became the fourth generation of Rahr family brewers. When he took over as the brewmaster in 1952, he continued to brew from the same recipe that had been in use before Prohibition. The only deviation came in late fall, when he would brew the

Jerry's Bar on Ceape Avenue in Oshkosh had a long association with Rahr Brewing. Here the Rahr sign comes down after the brewery closed in 1956.

annual bock beer for release in spring. It too was the same "dark-brown, mellow brew that has brought pleasure to Oshkosh folks for over seventy years." Something had to change.

In 1952, the brewery released beer in seven-ounce bottles simply labeled Rahr's Pale Beer. With that, Elk's Head was gone, at least in name. According to the brewmaster, the beer inside the bottle went unchanged. In fact, the Rahrs reached back even further. In 1953, in celebration of Oshkosh's centennial, Rahr Brewing released an all-malt beer. It was the first time since before Prohibition that a Winnebago County brewery made beer without corn or rice as part of the grist. The Rahrs were going out on their own terms.

Sales had plummeted. In 1954, Rahr produced just 5,683 barrels of beer. In 1955, it was down to 3,660 barrels. In the first half of 1956, the downward thrust continued to accelerate. On June 7, 1956, Blanche Rahr released a statement announcing the brewery would close at the end of the month. The tradition was over. Demolition of the brewery began in 1964. The homes that stand there now are part of a quiet neighborhood that gives no hint of its past. The only reminder is the street cutting through it named after the family that launched a brewery there in 1865.

MENASHA'S GEM

Christian Walter was sixteen when he left Germany in 1872. He reached Milwaukee later that year with five dollars left to his name. He was sixty-three and president of his own brewery when Prohibition stripped him of his avocation. For Walter, it must have been almost beyond belief—something like a nightmare. He would never emerge from it. Christian Walter died in 1932, five months before the repeal of Prohibition.

Christian Walter.

At Walter Brothers Brewing, they scrambled to regroup. Christian Walter's son John took over as brewery president. It was a job he did not want. It didn't help that the brewery was in such disrepair. It took nearly a year of renovation before Walter Brothers had its beer back on the market. Finally, in late June 1933, bottles of Walter Brothers Gold Label Beer were again ready for delivery. A year after that, John Walter sold his controlling interest in the brewery. Charles Kulnick added another notch to his brewery belt when he took over as general manager of Walter Brothers on August 1, 1934. Kulnick was sixty-three and had run Wisconsin breweries in Berlin and Manitowoc before arriving in Menasha. He was vice president of Kingsbury Breweries when he purchased a majority stake in Walter Brothers.

Kulnick's brief tenure at the brewery was relatively uneventful. His most significant act may have been the lease of the brewery's grain elevators and silos to Chilton Malting, forerunner of today's Briess Malt Company. The Chilton maltster would conduct a portion of its malting operations at the Walter Brothers site for the next twenty-five years. Kulnick continued the plant renovations that began with the end of Prohibition and focused the brewery on re-establishing its Menasha base. Kulnick had largely accomplished that by the time of his passing in 1938.

Over the next decade, the brewery went through a dizzying swirl of managerial and ownership changes. The presidency of the brewery swapped hands three times, and twice majority ownership shifted. For most breweries, that kind of flux was a sign of trouble. Not at Walter Brothers. Through it all, the brewery maintained a forward-moving constancy. The unvarying element at the center of it all was Walter H. Peirce. He married Christian Walter's daughter Mollie in 1900 and had been working for the Walter

Top, left: "K" as in Kulnick, a bottle label for a short-lived brand produced by Walter Brothers after Charles Kulnick became the brewery's president in 1934.

Top, right: A bar coaster from Walter Brothers. The brewery's telephone number 2 was just behind the Hotel Menasha's telephone number 1.

Bottom: Labels for the two main brands of Walter Brothers beer in the post-Prohibition period.

brothers ever since. During the volatile 1940s, Peirce's title changed almost annually from secretary to treasurer to vice president and president.

All that took place behind the scenes while the brewery dependably pumped out twelve to thirteen thousand barrels of beer each year. With the 1940s, Walter Brothers' production began to steadily tick upwards, due in large part to the introduction of Little Gem Pilsener in 1941. Gem was among the first Wisconsin beers packaged in seven-ounce bottles and almost immediately became one of the fastest growing brands of beer in the state. By the mid-1940s, Gem had replaced Gold Label as the brewery's flagship beer.

The success caught the attention of Appleton investor and meat market owner Charles A. Hopfensperger. Hopfensperger bought his way into the brewery in 1948 and took over as president in 1951. With that came a dramatic shift in approach. Prior to 1950, Walter Brothers had, for the most part, been content with its sales in Winnebago and Outagamie Counties. Now the brewery began to press out further. It was a tactic more and more small Wisconsin breweries were turning to. Their encounters away from home too often devolved into price wars.

In the early 1950s, brands such as Miller, Pabst and Schlitz demanded a premium price, about $3.40 a case. At the same time, beer from smaller Wisconsin breweries typically sold for $1.00 or so less. If a brewery was especially desperate—such as the Knapstein Brewery in New London or the Storck Brewery in Slinger—its beer would go for as little as $1.95 a case. That downward pricing spiral spelled a brewery's doom. Walter Brothers was drawn into the vortex.

The brewery began selling beer in places like Racine and Wisconsin Rapids. With sales of thirty thousand barrels of beer in 1951, the brewery was at its peak. But it paid a high price to get there. Volume was up, but profits were down. Walter Brothers took an aggressive approach to pricing, often selling its beer much cheaper than others. At times, the brewery was literally giving it away, offering two free bottles of beer in exchange for a newspaper coupon. In Sheboygan, Gem Pilsener was advertised as the "Lowest Priced Beer in Town." If that wasn't good enough, they'd give you four bottles free if you bought a case. Walter Brothers attempted to shake the "cheap beer" image by reformulating its recipe in 1953 and undertaking an ad campaign promising that the new Gem beer had "revived that old-fashioned, real beer character." It was too late for that. People weren't buying Gem based on its flavor, they were buying it based on price. Walter Brothers had gone as low as it could on that front.

Left: A mid-1940s tap knob from Walter Brothers.

Below: A tin-over-cardboard bar sign from around 1950.

Sales fell precipitously after the recipe changed. By the spring of 1956, desperation had set in. At some bottle shops, a case of low-priced Gem beer came with a free six-pack thrown in. Not even that revived the slumping sales. In June 1956, word began to leak out that the brewery would close. On June 27, Oshkosh Brewing took out a large ad in the *Twin-City News Record* to announce that Paul Laemmrich was now selling Chief Oshkosh Beer. Prior to that, Laemmrich had been head of sales for Walter Brothers in Neenah and Menasha. The pronouncement that followed was merely a formality. On June 29, 1956, Walter Brothers Brewing announced that it would close and that production had already been halted. For the first time in more than a century, Menasha would be a city without a brewery. The Walter Brothers brewery was purchased by the St. Patrick's congregation and razed in 1960.

PEOPLES POWER

It wasn't all doom and gloom. In Oshkosh, an entirely different story was playing out. After the deck was cleared of Prohibition's wreckage, Peoples Brewing found itself possessing a natural advantage. The brewery's cooperative ownership model insulated it from the problems plaguing so many of Wisconsin's smaller breweries.

With the tied-house system gone, local breweries were forced into competition with much larger breweries that distributed their brands nationally. When it came to promotion and advertising, few of the smaller breweries had the resources to make it a fair fight, so they resorted to cut-rate pricing to make their brands stand out. At the same time, the scale of production at a smaller brewery meant a higher unit price: it cost them more to produce their beer, and they received less for it. For most, it was an unwinnable game. In 1934, Wisconsin was home to more than eighty breweries. By 1954, almost half of those had closed. During that same period, Peoples grew its sales by 200 percent.

The formula for that success could not have been more basic: mine the local market for all it was worth. In Oshkosh, that meant selling beer in taverns. Peoples continued to enjoy the fruits of a tied-house type of patronage. Many of Oshkosh's tavern owners were also Peoples stockholders. They maintained a vested interest in keeping the brewery's beer flowing. Their reliable promotion was priceless, and Peoples paid nothing for it. The circumstance was similar when it came to packaged beer. Ownership of the brewery was widespread within its community. Folks picking up a case at the beer depot might as well buy the beer from the brewery they owned a piece of. With that kind of backing, Peoples didn't need to engage in price cutting. The brewery was never forced into going lower than the going rate to entice customers. The beer it was making for those customers was tailored to their tastes.

Oshkosh drinkers had a reputation for favoring beer that was malt-driven and somewhat sweeter. The beer coming out of Peoples Brewing was just that. Brewmaster Joseph Stier had been with Peoples since 1914. Coming out of Prohibition, Stier scrapped the brewery's old lineup and introduced a new beer named Wurtzer, a golden-hued beer that leaned on darker-kilned malts for its rich flavor. Wurtzer didn't quite fit the trend toward lighter, less flavorful beers, but it was exactly what Peoples customers were looking for. Over the course of the 1950s, the Wurtzer name would give way to the more simply branded Peoples Beer, but the liquid behind the label saw little change.

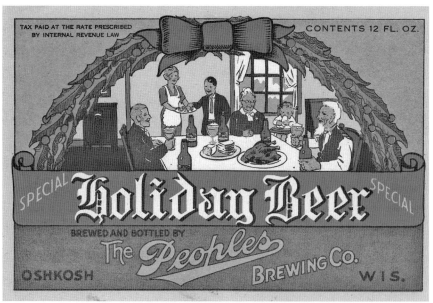

Top, left: A coaster frequently seen on bar tops in Oshkosh in the late 1930s.

Top, right: Holiday seasonal beers were popular in Winnebago County through much of the 1900s. This festive label was used by Peoples Brewing in the 1940s.

Bottom: A bar tray from Peoples showing the brewery's main brands in the 1940s.

That malty groove became the brewery's signature. Each spring, Peoples would release a strong bock beer made with Munich malt that delivered intense malt flavor and aromatics. Every December was greeted with Peoples Holiday Beer, another malt bomb brewed in limited quantities as a special treat for the brewery's customers. A singular departure from that theme came in 1937, when Peoples purchased the Old Derby Ale brand from the defunct Ripon Brewing Company. It was the only ale produced by a Winnebago County brewery in the post-Prohibition era. Above average in strength, Old Derby's bitter hop presence was in stark contrast to what drinkers expected from Peoples. It didn't take. By 1951, Old Derby Ale had been abandoned, and nobody seemed to miss it.

Production at the brewery rose steadily, from an average of fifteen thousand barrels in the 1930s to thirty-four thousand barrels by 1953. On the wings of that growth came improvements to every part of the brewery. George "Tuffy" Boeder started at Peoples in 1936. "A lot was done by hand back then," he said. "We had to label each bottle separately. If we did 30 barrels a day that was a lot." A new bottling line took care of that. By the early 1950s, Peoples regularly employed forty or more workers. At the end of the decade, the brewery began canning its beer. Peoples became a rare model of success among regional breweries. It was one among just a handful of small Wisconsin breweries that managed to remain prosperous. Another brewery in that select group stood right across the street.

CHIEF OSHKOSH

Hardly anybody referred to it as the Oshkosh Brewing Company anymore. It had become so identified with its flagship brand that people took to calling it the Chief Oshkosh Brewery. Nobody there minded. In fact, they encouraged it. No Winnebago County brewery had ever marketed so heavily as Oshkosh Brewing did in the years after Prohibition. The brewery advertised in print, on TV and radio and through an endless stream of tavern paraphernalia. Stamped on all of it was Chief Oshkosh.

The Menominee Indian Chief Oshkosh died in 1858. Most of the brewery's promotional material incorporated imagery of the chief based on an 1855 daguerreotype showing him wearing a beaver hat and tailcoat. But Chief Oshkosh wasn't used as a brand name until 1928, when the brewery released a near beer named Chief Oshkosh Special. After

A 1930s beer tray from the Oshkosh Brewing Company.

Prohibition, it turned into the real thing and became the brewery's flagship brand. They grew so enamored with the chief that brewery representatives took to saying he had posed for the 1855 daguerreotype during one of his many visits to the brew house. That was pure fiction. Oshkosh died years before the launch of any of the three breweries that merged in 1894 to form Oshkosh Brewing.

Chief Oshkosh grew into an iconic Wisconsin brand. It became the most widely known and best-selling beer ever produced by a Winnebago County brewery. It was distributed throughout Wisconsin and in parts of Illinois, Michigan and Minnesota. At a time when regional brands were being crushed by national brands, Chief Oshkosh sales grew year after year. During the ten months of 1933 when it was permitted to make real beer again, Oshkosh Brewing produced 39,024 barrels of Chief Oshkosh. By 1953, the brewery's internal records showed output had increased to over 60,000 barrels. No other brewery in the Fox Valley came close to that.

The brewery's strongest market remained Oshkosh. The growth of Peoples had a limiting effect, but the two breweries settled into a semi-peaceful coexistence. Peoples tended to have a slight edge on keg beer sales. Oshkosh Brewing had the advantage when it came to bottled beer. The brewery went hard in that direction. In 1937, Oshkosh Brewing was selling 22 percent of its beer in bottles. By 1949, bottled beer accounted for 63 percent of the brewery's sales. That same year, the brewery became the first in Winnebago County to can its beer. Oshkosh Brewing went through a series of different can shapes beginning with crowntainers and cone tops before settling on a standard flattop can in 1953.

The packaging was more diverse than the beer inside. The variety of beer styles the brewery had produced at the turn of the century had been reduced to variations on a single Chief Oshkosh theme. In comparison to the maltier Peoples Beer, Chief Oshkosh had a more assertive hop profile. They toned that down in 1950. The brewery introduced a new recipe that produced a lighter Chief Oshkosh designed to attract a broader audience. Sales of the beer jumped 28 percent. The only breaks from the pale lager routine came in the spring, with the release of the brewery's bock beer,

Above: A mid-century aerial view of the Oshkosh Brewing Company.

Right: The evolution of the Chief Oshkosh can from the 1949 crowntainer *(left)* to the flattop can of 1953.

and in late November, when Chief Oshkosh Holiday Beer came out. Both beers were stronger and a touch darker than the usual, but the base profile of each hued closely to that of the everyday Chief Oshkosh. The days of dark lager were long gone.

In May 1956, Oshkosh Brewing celebrated its ninetieth anniversary with a four-day party on the brewery grounds. More than five thousand people turned out. The partnership formed by August Horn and Leonhardt Schwalm in 1866 had been passed along to a third generation. Leonhardt

Schwalm's grandson Arthur Schwalm was now the brewery president. August Horn's grandson Earl Horn was the vice president. From the vantage point of those heady days in May, it looked as if it would all keep rolling on and on. There was no end in sight.

10

1960–1972

ROADS TO NOWHERE

SCHLITZED

The undoing of the Oshkosh Brewing Company took nearly a decade. It began in early 1961, when Arthur Schwalm and Earl Horn entered negotiations to sell their majority stake in the brewery to David V. Uihlein (pronounced EE-Line). In June 1961, the talks stalled when Arthur Schwalm suffered a heart attack and died. But by the end of summer, a deal had been struck. The announcement came on August 16, 1961. David Uihlein had purchased the shares of Horn and Schwalm and would take over Oshkosh Brewing as its new president. The news landed with a thud.

Uihlein's motivation for buying the brewery was immediately called into question. He was a member of the family that owned the controlling interest in Schlitz, America's second largest brewery. People in Oshkosh speculated that Uihlein was acting on behalf of Schlitz in an effort to grab the local market. The suspicion was well founded. Though it would be years before it was revealed, Uihlein's plan did include Schlitz taking over Oshkosh Brewing. But there was a hitch. Uihlein's scheme had not been approved by the board of directors of Schlitz. He was operating unilaterally. The maneuver derailed when he placed his newly acquired brewery at the doorstep of his cousin Robert Uihlein, who had just been named president of Schlitz. "I didn't want that tea kettle rammed down my throat on the first day of the job," Robert Uihlein would later say. "We didn't buy it, but I

David Uihlein.

had to spend an entire Saturday afternoon at my house convincing David that his brewery would never make it."

David Uihlein managed to keep all of that to himself. When it came time to make the big announcement, he spoke of aspirations. "This is the fulfillment of a dream that has been mine since I was a boy—to own and operate my own brewery," Uihlein said. It was all downhill from there. Over the next eight years, Uihlein made a series of blunders the equal of his opening gambit. Each would drive the brewery further down the hole. Uihlein was shielded by his wealth. Others would suffer the consequences of his feckless miscalculations.

After settling in, Uihlein put his own stamp on the brewery. Within a year of taking charge, he changed both the Chief Oshkosh label and recipe. The label was in keeping with his vision of Winnebago County as a land of leisure. The new recipe was all about expediency. Uihlein replaced the corn grits used in Chief Oshkosh with a brewer's corn syrup named NuBru. At the same time, hop extracts began taking the place of actual hops.

Uihlein knew what he was doing. He was a diploma brewer experienced in every facet of the process. His brewmaster in Oshkosh was even more adept. Wilbur Strottman was a highly experienced and knowledgeable brewer who had taught brewing science at the Siebel Institute in Chicago. Together, Uihlein and Strottman continually tinkered with Chief Oshkosh, moving it further away from its traditional base in favor of more extracts and a wider array of adjuncts. It was a cheaper, more efficient way to brew, but the changes hadn't gone unnoticed. Sales dropped off. Uihlein countered the decline by expanding distribution and selling Chief Oshkosh at bargain prices. Initially, the tactic worked. Production rebounded in 1963 back to almost fifty-nine thousand barrels, which was on par with the brewery's output prior to the arrival of Uihlein. But the reformulated Chief Oshkosh didn't take in the new markets either. By the end of 1965, production was down 14 percent.

Inside the brewery, the strain was evident. Internal memos show Uihlein taking his frustrations out on his subordinates, demanding they improve their performance. Some took that as a sign of his determination. "Uihlein did everything he could do to keep the brewery in business," said Harold

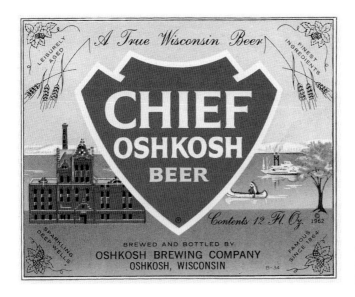

The Chief Oshkosh label after its 1962 redesign.

Kriz, a veteran employee of the brewery who became its general manager under Uihlein. Kriz's sentiments are backed by the equipment upgrades and increases to the advertising budget made during Uihlein's tenure. Others were less impressed. Assistant brewmaster Gerald Kundinger, who had worked at the brewery since 1937, said Uihlein ran the business as if it were a "hobby." Among the disaffected was a man whose favor Uihlein paid dearly for losing.

In 1961, the treasurer of the brewery, Lorenz "Shorty" Kuenzl had learned that Uihlein was attempting to buy his way in. Kuenzl was the grandson of the brewery's first brewmaster, Lorenz Kuenzl, and had been with Oshkosh Brewing since the end of Prohibition. Kuenzl made a failed bid to block the purchase by Uihlein and after the sale maintained his position on the brewery's board of directors. He was now the only board member with a familial link to the brewery's origin. Uihlein wanted him gone, and he got what he wanted. Kuenzl retired in 1963, but he didn't go quietly.

Kuenzl was well-liked by area tavern owners. He had led the brewery's sales force and played a significant role in the dramatic growth of Chief Oshkosh Beer in the 1950s. Kuenzl was set to do it all over again. Upon leaving the brewery, he purchased Lee Beverage of Oshkosh, a small beer distributorship. Kuenzl was joined by his sons John and Lorenz, who was nicknamed "Bud" and had also worked at Oshkosh Brewing. The Kuenzl family grew the distributorship into an imposing force. The rise of Lee Beverage occurred in tandem with Oshkosh Brewing losing its hometown market. For Kuenzl, the victory was tinged with melancholy. He never relinquished his stake in the brewery he and his family had helped to build.

Those shares of stock Kuenzl owned were worth less every day. At the end of 1965, it was evident the brewery could no longer survive on the tarnished reputation of Chief Oshkosh. Uihlein wasn't giving up. He acquired brands from three defunct Wisconsin breweries and in 1966 began producing Badger Brew, originally made by Effinger Brewing of Baraboo; Liebrau, a failed brand from Two Rivers Beverage; and Rahr's Beer of the recently shuttered Rahr Brewing of Green Bay. The beer Uihlein was putting behind those labels may have been Chief Oshkosh. Brewing logs from the period show no recipe variations for the individual brands. Each brew was produced from the same adulterated template.

It hardly mattered. By the close of 1967, the brewery was cratering. Annual production fell below fifty thousand barrels for the first time since 1951. In 1968, it dropped to just forty thousand barrels, the brewery's lowest output since the end of Prohibition. Uihlein had given up and was spending more and more time tending to his affairs in Milwaukee. When his father, Joseph Uihlein, died in 1968, it opened the way for David Uihlein to sell his stake in Oshkosh Brewing and take his place on the board of directors

The eight-hundred-pound terracotta emblem above the entrance to the Oshkosh Brewing Company.

at Schlitz. There Uihlein helped to conduct the most catastrophic brewery failure in American history.

On June 30, 1969, a coterie of longtime brewery employees announced their purchase of Oshkosh Brewing. The group, working as Hometown Brewery, Inc., was led by Harold Kriz, who would be the new president of the brewery. It was a valiant effort, but what was set in motion in 1961 was irreversible eight years later. Chief Oshkosh had become a brand synonymous with low quality. One reviewer described it as a beer with no redeeming value. In 1970, production sank to twenty-seven thousand barrels. The last batch of Chief Oshkosh was brewed on September 9, 1971. A month later, the brewery was closed. There were more humiliations to come.

On November 5, 1971, Peoples Brewing announced it had purchased and would produce the Chief Oshkosh brand. It was the culmination of the battle that began when William Glatz and Oshkosh Brewing had drawn the ire of local saloon keepers in the 1890s. The magnificent brewery that had been William Glatz's crowning achievement was left to molder. Beginning in 1986, after it had been set on fire and routinely vandalized, the brewery was demolished. What remains is the eight-hundred-pound terracotta Chief Oshkosh emblem that hovered over the brewery's entrance. It's now encased at the entrance to the Oshkosh Public Museum.

Last Call

Peoples Brewing cut an unusually steady path through the turbulent 1960s. The period was a devastating one for America's regional brewers. By the end of the decade, 80 percent of U.S. beer was being produced by just 10 breweries. The other 144 American breweries were left fighting over scraps. Just 15 breweries remained in Wisconsin. In terms of output, Peoples ranked twelfth on the Wisconsin list. But unlike most of the others, a cloud of imminent doom had not settled over Peoples. Sales of Peoples Beer stayed healthy throughout the 1960s. The brewery's annual production ranged from twenty-five to thirty thousand barrels. The main focus had always been the sale of beer in local taverns. The tried and true was still paying dividends. And so it remained until April 14, 1970, when everything began to change all at once.

The April 15 *Oshkosh Northwestern* headline was like an explosion: "Black Businessmen Buy Peoples Brewery." The group was led by Theodore Mack, a Milwaukee insurance agent and former employee of Pabst Brewing. A year

Items such as this lighted sign from the 1960s were once seen as having little value. Today they are worth hundreds of dollars.

earlier, Mack and company had made a failed attempt to purchase the Blatz brand from Pabst. When they were outbid on Blatz, they looked elsewhere. In October 1969, they found people at a brewery in Oshkosh willing to deal. Now, six months later, it was up to the shareholders of Peoples to decide whether or not to sell out.

Ownership of Peoples had remained diversified. None of the 160 shareholders held anything approaching a majority stake. Approximately 135 of those shareholders turned up at the brewery on April 14 to decide on the offer tendered by Mack. An overwhelming majority of 80 percent voted to take it. Later that evening, Fred Gordy, the Milwaukee developer who brokered the deal, remarked, "It was a nice operating and profitable brewery." His use of the past tense would prove to be unintentionally predictive.

The trouble began with a specious claim published by the *Milwaukee Sentinel* that management posts at the brewery would be filled by blacks and that the policy would be to hire black workers to replace whites. That didn't play well in Oshkosh, where 99 percent of the population was white. Sales of Peoples Beer immediately tanked. Grant Peterson, a route driver for Peoples, reported that his deliveries decreased by half. The ugly reaction was distilled in the odious comment of a south side Oshkosh bartender who said, "It was good beer 'til the nigger came." Mack spent the next two weeks quelling the uproar and assuring people that the brewery's twenty-one employees were secure in their positions. The endless rounds of appeasement wearied him. By the end of the month, Mack's tone had changed. He was done placating racists. "Myself and Oshkosh are very much on the spot," Mack told a reporter at the end of April. "This is regarded as one of the most bigoted cities in the country, north and south. If sales are down it will be a black eye on Oshkosh, not on me. I can hold up my end. It's a matter of whether Oshkosh can hold up its end."

That put the events of the past weeks in perspective. An outpouring of support for Mack's cause followed. He needed it. The purchase was contingent upon a $390,000 loan that would not come through until the group had secured $200,000 in operating capital. Mack planned to sell stock to raise the additional funds. When shares went on sale in July, people in Oshkosh lined up. "We have had an extremely good response in Oshkosh," Mack said at the end of the first week of the stock being made available. By mid-September, Mack had raised the required capital. He moved his family to Oshkosh and became something of a local celebrity. Sales of Peoples Beer rebounded.

On October 10, 1970, they threw a party. The *Oshkosh Northwestern* described it as an open house "to celebrate new management and to salute what Peoples' President Ted Mack predicted will be an unlimited future of expansion and growth." Along with a host of state and local officials, some seven thousand people turned out. During the ribbon-cutting ceremony, Mack delivered an emotional speech, telling the crowd, "In these days of confrontations, you make a pretty picture standing there black, white and brown." Mack had transformed the rancorous beginning into something both he and the community could be proud of.

The good feelings carried over into 1971. Peoples expanded its distribution into Madison, Milwaukee and Racine. Production rose correspondingly, returning to the high levels of the mid-1950s. Mack's fame was growing. He was constantly sought after for speaking engagements. His story received national press coverage, with Peoples invariably described as "the nation's first black-owned brewery." It made for a good story, but it wasn't accurate. Brewery historian Doug Hoverson has discovered that the Sunshine Brewing Company of Reading, Pennsylvania, earned that distinction in 1969.

If Mack's goal had been to run a thriving regional brewery, he would have attained it by the summer of 1971. That wasn't his goal. Mack wanted to distribute nationally, focusing on urban markets, where he thought his story would attract customers eager to support a black-owned business. Peoples Beer was sent to Indianapolis, Los Angeles and Memphis. It was a gamble. Lacking the sales infrastructure needed to introduce an unknown product into far-flung markets, Mack was reliant on word of mouth and media reports that focused on him to motivate potential customers. It wasn't enough. None of the new markets proved hospitable. When three trucks carrying Peoples Beer were sent to Gary, Indiana, they were impounded by local officials who alleged that the brewery was acting as its own distributor in violation of state law. In Milwaukee, retailers complained about the premium price of Peoples. "It's strictly price," said one Milwaukee liquor store owner. "If it weren't for the price the beer would be doing much better." As problems mounted, Mack brooded. "It seems like there's a national conspiracy to kill Peoples Brewing Company," he said. "Everywhere we go we run into the white power structure."

At the same time, sales of Peoples Beer continued growing in the Fox Valley and in smaller Wisconsin cities like Ripon and Whitewater. Mack, who had a sociology degree, was flummoxed. "It just doesn't make sense the way the markets are polarizing and where our sales are getting a good reception," he said. "I've been studying human behavior all my life, but since I have been in the brewery business I have found out I don't know a damned thing about it." Though edifying, success in the smaller markets didn't provide the returns Mack needed to service the debt incurred upon purchasing the brewery.

By the autumn of 1971, the brewery was faltering. Mack was running out of money and options. The brewery pulled back from Milwaukee and concentrated resources locally. In November 1971, Peoples acquired the brands of the recently failed Oshkosh Brewing and began producing Chief Oshkosh Beer. It was no remedy for the brewery's fiscal woes. A year earlier, Mack had assumed control of an obscure but profitable brewery. He had turned it into a nationally known entity and in the process destroyed it. It had been a high-risk undertaking. Had it succeeded, Mack would have been lauded. Instead, he found himself caught in the midst of a very public failure.

By the end of 1971, Peoples Brewing had stopped making payments on its bank loan. The brewery was deep in the red. Mack continued to say publicly that everything was fine, but behind the scenes, there was a maelstrom. In March 1972, Mack's fellow board members called him to the carpet for his lack of candor in keeping them abreast of the brewery's "financial crisis." Mack pivoted away from the failing urban strategy and began trying to secure government contracts for supplying beer to the military. That plan fared no better. In October 1972, the IRS filed tax liens against Peoples for failure to pay excise taxes on the sale of its beer.

Mack flailed. He intimated that he might move the brewery to Alabama or Nigeria. He sued the U.S. government for not awarding Peoples a military

Right: From early 1972, Chief Oshkosh gets the Peoples treatment.

Below: Peoples Brewing shortly after its closing in 1972.

contract. After the case was dismissed, he said he would appeal to the Supreme Court. These were the final convulsions of a brewery in its death throes. They stopped making beer at Peoples Brewing in the third week of October 1972. The brewery's workforce was laid off. Winnebago County's last remaining brewery was closed. It was demolished in July 1974.

AFTERMATH

In 1972, Winnebago County was without a brewery for the first time in 123 years. For something that had been so central to its cultural life, the history of those breweries was forgotten with startling swiftness. The disregard is especially surprising in light of the county's long practice of preserving the memories of its past. Few Midwestern counties of its size have been so well chronicled. Largely absent from those recollections have been its breweries.

Take, for example, the brewery that stood in the heart of the village of Butte des Morts. The history of the small village has inspired a wealth of documentation, but the brewery that had been there is missing from almost all of it. This despite the fact that the descendants of the last owner, Frederick Bogk, continued on in the village, operating taverns there into the 1950s. In Winneconne, the memory lapse was just as thorough. With the death of Theodore Yager in 1899 came one of the last, brief mentions of Yager's Winneconne Brewery. After that, the thread was lost. In Neenah, the forgetting may have been more volitional. Neenah's early history was told from the viewpoint of its dominant class. They tended to support the temperance movement. For them, Neenah's brewery was a memory happily buried. In Menasha and Oshkosh, it was hardly better. Their numerous pre-Prohibition breweries were consigned to obscurity. The more recent breweries appeared destined for the same fate. City histories written in the aftermath of the breweries that closed in the 1950s and 1970s make only cursory mention of the vital role they once played. Yet links to that fading past were still all around. Taverns built by those breweries continued to be popular gathering points in almost every Winnebago County community long after the breweries were gone.

The nasty decay of Oshkosh Brewing's hulking plant stretched into the 1980s. What it represented was eyed with disdain. "It's just an old brewery building that's got some old vats," said Oshkosh's director of community development shortly before the brewery was demolished. There are two remaining intact brewery structures in Winnebago County that predate Prohibition: the Horn and Schwalm Brewery, built in 1879, and the bottling house of Peoples Brewing, built in 1913. Both are located on the south side of Oshkosh. Neither bears designation of its former status.

What was not lost has been preserved through the work of hobbyists interested in history and drawn to collecting brewery memorabilia. They refer to it as "breweriana." For Menasha collector John Fritsch, the urge to know more about his hometown's breweries came early. "I was into it from the start," Fritsch said. "Even as a kid, I'd go around talking to old people asking them questions about what they remembered. I'd go through any old stuff people thought was junk trying to find things." At the time, he was one of the few who thought discarded tap knobs, bar signs or beer bottles were worth saving. Many of the Menasha breweriana items Fritsch saved are now thought to be the only surviving pieces of their kind.

Fritsch wasn't able to save everything he found. Growing up in the early 1950s, he heard about the old beer cellars that existed beneath the abandoned Menasha Brewing Company. Fritsch had to see them. He befriended Helen Schreiter, a member of the Winz family that ran the brewery before Prohibition. Schreiter still lived next door to the old brewery. In the basement of her home was a passageway that led into the

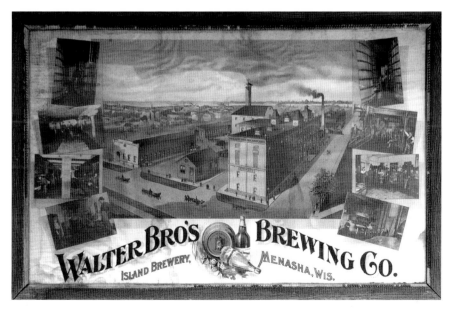

A rare piece of breweriana from the early 1900s.

A rare pre-Prohibition wooden sign produced by the Meyercord Company of Chicago for Rahr Brewing.

beer tunnels where the brewery had aged its beer. Some of those tunnels dated back to the 1850s. Schreiter, taken with the boy's enthusiasm, allowed Fritsch to enter the cellars through her basement to explore them. "They were incredible," said Fritsch. "And the stonework was just beautiful. It's such a shame that it's gone."

Ron Akin's interest in preserving Oshkosh's brewing history developed just as the last of the city's breweries was closing. It began after his sons Dan and David took up beer-can collecting in the early 1970s. As Akin helped his sons grow their collections, he became fascinated with the items they were finding. "So, I became a collector too, collecting anything related to any of the closed Oshkosh breweries," Akin said. "Those breweries began in the middle of the 1800s. There was so little information available on them. I wanted to know more. Collecting breweriana became part of that and as I learned more, I discovered how important the breweries were to the history of Oshkosh."

Akin, a retired University of Wisconsin–Oshkosh professor, was happy to share what he was discovering. He began writing and giving talks about the history of brewing in Oshkosh. His research culminated in 2012 with the publication of *The Breweries of Oshkosh, Their Rise and Fall*, which Akin coauthored. "One of the reasons we wanted to do that is that we wanted our town to know the facts of what happened here. We're proud of that contribution," Akin said. Akin's collection of Oshkosh breweriana is the most complete in existence. He hopes it will continue to serve as a reminder of the history it represents. "My dream is that when I'm gone that this collection will stay together in or near Oshkosh," Akin said. "I don't want it divided up going out in pieces across the country. Some of those pieces would never be seen again."

The efforts of people like John Fritsch and Ron Akin to preserve Winnebago County's brewing history had a secondary effect they never anticipated. It helped to inform what was to come. After a twenty-year absence, brewing returned to Winnebago County. The people who led the revival were being made keenly aware of the lineage they would be stewards of.

11

BUILDING A NEW SCENE

SOMETHING IN THE WATER

Homebrewing in Winnebago County became wildly popular with the onset of Prohibition. When the breweries began closing in 1919, people from all walks of life started making their own beer. In 1972, all of the county's breweries had again run dry. The circumstance was different, but the reaction of some people wasn't. They turned to homebrewing. Homebrewing was made illegal when Prohibition ended. The overreach was addressed in 1977, when Representative William A. Steiger of Oshkosh introduced a bill that would legalize making beer at home for personal consumption. President Jimmy Carter signed the bill into law in 1978. Winnebago County homebrewers began coming out of the woodwork. The movement gathered momentum all through the 1980s.

In 1991, the county's first homebrewing club, the Society of Oshkosh Brewers, was formed. Referring to themselves as the SOBs, the club drew in members from across the county and beyond. "Upholding Wisconsin's Brewing Tradition" became the SOBs' motto. The club's logo featured an illustration of the stovepipe hat worn by Chief Oshkosh in the old trademark of the Oshkosh Brewing Company. The influence of the past also showed in the beer. In the 1850s, Winnebago County brewers discovered that the local water was especially well suited for brewing dark, malt-forward styles of beer. The new wave of homebrewers recovered that lost truth. Steve Rehfeldt moved from Colorado to Oshkosh in 1995 and joined the SOBs. "The home brewers here produced great beers," Rehfeldt said. "They brewed a lot of

Kevin Bowen, head brewer at Fox River, on the mash tun deck during a group brew with members of the Society of Oshkosh Brewers.

lagers and malty, dark ales." More than a century earlier, the same could have been said about the Loescher brothers or Theodore Yager.

As the SOBs grew, so did their influence on the local beer culture. Members inhabited area taverns calling for something more substantial than the bland, industrial lager that had become commonplace. Taverns like Oblio's Lounge in Oshkosh and Club Tavern in Menasha responded, bringing in beers that were part of this new thing called micro-brew. The time was right for brewing to return to Winnebago County.

CHIEF OSHKOSH RED LAGER AND THE MID-COAST BREWING COMPANY

In the summer of 1991, there came a new beer with a familiar-sounding name. Aside from that name, there was no connection between Chief Oshkosh Red Lager and the Chief Oshkosh Beer of old. The new beer was the creation of Jeff Fulbright, president and brewer for the Mid-Coast Brewing Company of Oshkosh.

Fulbright was a restaurateur inspired by the early micro-brew movement. In 1989, he had gone to Chicago to train as a brewer at the Siebel Institute. There, he began working up a recipe for an all-malt beer that he hoped to make the main brand for the brewery he sought to establish. The recipe Fulbright developed produced a malt-forward lager with a distinctive red hue. "Chief Oshkosh Red Lager was born at Siebel," Fulbright said. He returned from Chicago and began planning his brewery. Fulbright's initial thought was to build a brewery in Oshkosh. Then he met Jim Koch, brewer of Samuel Adams beer. Koch had appraised the situation in Wisconsin and knew the state had surplus brewing capacity. Koch urged Fulbright to have his beer made at an existing brewery instead of building his own. Fulbright heeded the advice and contracted with Stevens Point Brewery. In May 1991, Chief Oshkosh Red Lager went into production.

In June 1991, Fulbright's beer hit the market. It had much in common with the Vienna-style lagers popular in Winnebago County in the latter half of the 1800s. But in the 1990s, it was unlike almost anything else. It was the first widely distributed beer branded as a red lager and the first American craft beer packaged in cans. In its immediate wake would come a legion of so-called red beers, but it would take decades before craft beer packaged in cans was embraced. When it happened, brewers adopted Fulbright's messaging that cans are better for the environment and better for the beer. But when Fulbright first introduced those concepts, they were a much tougher sell. "The idea that great beer doesn't come in a can hurt me," he said.

What poured from those cans was even more difficult for some to accept. "I went to all the taverns," Fulbright said. "I'd go in and have some old-geezer tavern owner yelling at me, 'I can't sell that dark shit!' " Beyond the narrow confines of the corner bar, though, Fulbright found a more appreciative audience. Craft beer spawned a new beer journalism that was about more than just the business side of brewing. People were writing about flavor, and they had high praise for Chief Oshkosh Red Lager. Mike Bosak, of *All About Beer*, wrote that it was "just delightful." Charlie Papazian described it in *Zymurgy* as "a pleasantly great beer." Michael Jackson, the doyen of beer writers, penned a glowing review, noting its "unapologetic, robust sweetness" and "delicate hint of hop."

Chief Oshkosh Red Lager was catching on. The original retailers were clustered in Winnebago, Outagamie and Fond du Lac Counties. "We sold in three counties what we thought we'd sell in thirteen," Fulbright said. By

Right: Chief Oshkosh Red Lager was the first American craft beer packaged in cans. Consumer resistance prompted Mid-Coast Brewing to also package the beer in bottles.

Below: An early promotional flyer for Chief Oshkosh Red Lager from 1992 touting the benefits of packaging quality beer in cans.

149

the end of 1992, the beer was available throughout the state. A year later, distribution expanded into much of the Midwest. But the rapid growth also planted the seeds of an equally rapid demise. The broad distribution outstripped Fulbright's financial capabilities. The gap between production costs and return on sales left Mid-Coast with an ongoing cash deficit.

More problematic was the attention Fulbright was getting from large breweries eager to capitalize on his innovations. In 1993, Miller Brewing, under the guise of a satellite brand, introduced Leinenkugel's Red Lager. To say the beers were similar would be an understatement. "You could hardly tell the difference between the two," Fulbright said. Fulbright found it impossible to compete with Miller's massive distribution network and advertising budget. "When Leinenkugel's moved in, my distributors lost interest," Fulbright said. "We started getting killed. It was a tsunami." In 1994, Chief Oshkosh Red Lager won a silver medal at the World Beer Championships. But by then, it was over. "Basically, we ran out of money," Fulbright said. "The big guy won. We didn't stand a chance." Mid-Coast Brewing ceased operations in early 1995. As of this writing, Jeff Fulbright is planning the launch of a new brewery in Oshkosh.

FOX RIVER BREWING COMPANY

1501 Arboretum Drive, Oshkosh

There hadn't been a brewery built in Winnebago County since 1913. That changed in the summer of 1995, when a new brewery began going up in Oshkosh. This new brewery was not like the breweries people remembered. This one had more in common with the 1850s than the 1950s. Like the older breweries, the new one was built on the river. And like those of old, this one was of modest size and designed to make small batches of beer for the community surrounding it. The brewery's name would tie it to its place.

Fox River Brewing Company began production of its first beer on November 18, 1995. That beer was a lager. But the people behind this brewery were as different as can be from the lager-brewing immigrants of old. Brothers Jay, Joe and John Supple hailed from Oshkosh. Their family had been in the restaurant business since the late 1960s. Fox River would open as a brewpub with the restaurant side of the operation named Fratellos. The Supples had a handle on that. When it came to brewing, though, "We

Fox River Brewing Company on the Fox River.

could drink beer, but we couldn't make beer," said Jay Supple. "We thought, if we're going to do a brewery, how do we do this right? That's when we hooked up with Rob."

Rob LoBreglio, co-owner of Madison's Great Dane Pub & Brewing, signed on as a consultant. He even brought along a brewer. Al Bunde was an Eau Claire native who had recently abandoned his career as a manufacturing engineer. Jovial and gregarious, Bunde fit right in at the helm of the new brew house. "It worked out beautifully," Jay Supple said. "Having these guys come in from Madison made it a smooth, almost seamless transition." Transitioning customers to more flavorful beer came next. Fox River's all-malt beers were in stark contrast to the fizzy, light lagers that had become the norm. "It will take some educating to get people used to the flavors," Bunde conceded. Yet he was adamant about the virtues. "It will be the freshest, highest quality beer you can get."

The timing was right. By the end of 1996, Fox River had produced over one thousand barrels of beer and was the fourteenth largest of Wisconsin's thirty-two breweries. The Supples were encouraged. In 1997, they built a second brewpub in Appleton and began bottling Fox River Golden Ale. It had been twenty-five years since a Winnebago County brewery had its beer on store shelves. "At the time, craft brewing wasn't what it is today," Jay Supple said. "We'd just do it ourselves. We'd go into grocery stores and make cold calls with our beer. At that point, you could still do something like that."

In 1998, Bunde left Oshkosh to help launch Stout Brothers Public House, a brewpub in Milwaukee. Steve Lonsway took over as head brewer. Lonsway

Left to right: John, Joe and Jay Supple in the brewhouse at Fox River.

had been running a homebrew shop in Appleton before coming to Fox River. He made the most of the opportunity. During Lonsway's tenure, the brewery won multiple awards for its beer. Fox River grew into the second largest brewpub in the state and was selling more beer off-premise than any other Wisconsin brewpub.

The momentum led to the Supple Group branching out into development projects in Madison and Oshkosh, and the launch of new restaurants in Appleton, Green Bay and Milwaukee. The brewery became just a part of a much larger business. After Lonsway left in 2002 to open what is now Stone Arch Brewpub in Appleton, a Boston brewer named Brian Allen was hired on. Under Allen, Fox River returned to its brewpub roots. Distribution was discontinued. The focus became making beer for the Appleton and Oshkosh brewpubs and the various establishments managed by the Supple Group. In the brew house, it was a period of relative stasis that incubated the next phase of growth.

Allen left Fox River in 2009, going to Springfield, Missouri, where he helped launch Mother's Brewing Company. Allen's influence, though, was lasting. He had introduced a fruit beer named Blü that would play an important role in the brewery's future. Allen had also trained the young brewer who would replace him. Kevin Bowen was only twenty-six when he took over as brewmaster, but he already had almost seven years of professional brewing experience. Bowen racked up a couple of prestigious World Beer Cup awards that helped to reignite interest in the brewery. The Supples decided it was time to get Fox River back into circulation.

"We were starting to see all these beers from other Wisconsin breweries going on the shelf in our area," Jay Supple said. "I'm like 'Hey, what are we doing here? We're the local guy.' I really felt we had too good of a product, too good of a name. We should be on the shelf. We said if we're going to do this, let's go out and get a bottling line and let's do production. Let's jump into it. Let's do it the right way." The new bottling line went in at the Appleton brewpub. The bottles that came out of it, more often than not, were filled with the fruit beer Allen had introduced, now labeled Blü Bobber. It became, as Jay Supple calls it, Fox River's rock-star beer. Production rose with the burgeoning popularity of Blü. In 2017, Fox River produced almost three thousand barrels of beer, the most the brewery has made in a single year.

"It's going to be interesting for us to see how far we go," Jay Supple said. "That's what we're trying to figure out. How far can we drive this? We're not interested in conquering how many different states, we're saying let's own as much as we can of this area here." For more than one hundred years, that has been a recipe for success for Winnebago County breweries. The small brewery on the Fox River has led to the renewal of a tradition thought to have been lost.

BARE BONES BREWERY

4362 County Hwy S, Oshkosh

In 2014, Dan and Patti Dringoli began making plans to put a brewery where there had never been a brewery before. The unlikely parcel the couple had in mind was just over the Oshkosh city line in the town of Oshkosh. The township had never had a legal brewery. In fact, the town of Oshkosh was among the first in Winnebago County to vote itself dry in the decade leading up to Prohibition. It was time to exorcise that old demon. There could be no better place to do it. The land at the intersection of County Highways S and Y is in the old hopyard region, just south of where Silas Allen planted the county's first hopyards in the late 1840s. In an era defined by hop-forward beers, there was something especially fitting about a new brewery going in where hops had long ago been king.

"It was a pipe dream before we found this location," Dan Dringoli said. "But when we found this, it seemed like it all fell into place." Dan had done some homebrewing before starting the brewery, but the couple earned their living running a property damage restoration business. When they were forced to relocate that business, they decided to include a brewery in their plans for the new location. "It just so happened we were going to be right on the Wiouwash Trail," Dan said. "We thought, that kind of thing would marry well with craft beer. There's that connection between peddle biking and breweries. I love this location. Coming here is what made us take the leap."

Leap they did, learning as they went. "Before that opening day, I had never even poured a beer from behind a bar," Patti said. "I was like a deer in headlights." The first beer had been brewed on July 16, 2015, on a new fifteen-barrel system. Within a couple of months, Bare Bones beer was pouring in taverns throughout the county and into Northeastern Wisconsin. After the acquisition of a portable bottling line in 2016, the brewery established its presence on area store shelves. The packaging evolved in early 2017, when

Bare Bones hired a mobile canning unit and became the first Winnebago County brewery to can its beer in more than twenty years.

The brewery's taproom has been where Bare Bones is best represented. Bare Bones wasn't just a name, it was a concept the Dringolis wanted to incorporate at their taproom in a way that would facilitate an atmosphere of conviviality. "Our 'Bare Bones' idea really came from the fact that we wanted to get people back in touch with each other," Patti said. "To unplug from their phones and TVs and get back to the basics of face to face conversation, remembering the fun of board games and meeting new people."

The initial flight of beers reflected the down-to-earth atmosphere. The Dringolis hired Fond du Lac homebrewer Lyle Hari as their head brewer. Hari's original brews were based on familiar styles—a cream ale, an amber ale and a porter were among them. After Hari departed in early 2016 for a position with a Florida brewery, the beer at Bare Bones grew more adventurous. R.J. Nordlund took over as head brewer in March 2016. He came from Michigan, where he had worked at several breweries, including Founders. Nordlund brought with him a love of hops.

The recipes he developed at Bare Bones reflected his passion. Nordlund produced a lineup of hop-forward ales including Dog Daze, an imperial

Dan and Patti Dringoli in their taproom at Bare Bones Brewery.

IPA that became the brewery's best-known beer. In 2018, Nordlund returned to his hometown of Montague, Michigan, to open a brewery of his own. Oshkosh brewing veteran Jody Cleveland took over brewing duties. Cleveland had come up through the homebrew ranks and had worked as an assistant brewer at both Bare Bones and Fox River Brewing. "This is still a young brewery and we're all really excited about what we're doing," Cleveland said. "I think we're in a good position to create something special here. This is just going to keep on developing."

The leap Dan and Patti Dringoli took has put them in a place where they're happy to be. "It's so much fun," Patti said. "We have a great group of people that come in. I love seeing our customers." It's been equally gratifying for Dan. "I think it's been everything we expected and more," he said. "It's been an amazing journey so far."

LION'S TAIL BREWING COMPANY

116 South Commercial Street, Neenah

"I was addicted," said Alex Wenzel. "It was all I thought about." Those words are even more fraught with ruin when they come from the mouth of a chemical engineer. But Wenzel's addiction was more or less benign. He was addicted to homebrewing. The most recent breweries launched in Winnebago County have been a direct outgrowth of the homebrewing movement that began surging after 2010. Wenzel's story epitomizes that of homebrewers turned professional and the ethos that informs their breweries and the beer they produce.

By the time Wenzel got around to homebrewing in 2012, he had already been a chemical engineer for fifteen years. "It was a pretty successful career, but not much fun," he said. A number of his work associates were avid homebrewers. Wenzel thought he'd try it. He was immediately hooked. In the evenings, after he and his wife, Kristin, had put their two children to bed, Wenzel would head to the basement and begin brewing. "It was one of those things where you think to yourself, how could I not have started doing this sooner? I just couldn't stop." Wenzel said. "At some point when you make three, four batches a week, you can't get your friends to drink enough beer, so it has to go down the drain just so you can keep brewing and continue learning." Wenzel needed to get out of the basement.

Alex Wenzel in the taproom at Lion's Tail Brewing.

In August 2014, Alex and Kristin decided his hobby had to become his livelihood. The transition was brisk. Lion's Tail Brewing held its grand opening on November 20, 2015. The taproom was packed. You'd have never guessed this was the same city that once embraced the temperance movement. Neenah's new brewery was in the historic Equitable Reserve Association building in the heart of downtown. The licensing for Wenzel's brew house was still being processed, so he produced his initial batches of beer at the nearby Appleton Beer Factory. It was the first of many collaborations Wenzel would partake in.

Wenzel's homebrewing roots have remained in evidence. Experimentation and variety are the benchmarks of his brewery. In less than three years, Wenzel has made more than 40 different beers at Lion's Tail. "I'm committed to doing at least 12 new beers every year," he said. "It's hard to do, but this place is never going to be a big regional brewery with all kinds of volume out in distribution. I'd love for this to be a destination where people go to try new things and come back, again and again, to see what we're up to next."

The first Lion's Tail beer to grab the public's attention was Kula Wheat, a golden wheat ale fermented on fresh pineapples Wenzel and his family shucked by hand. The laborious process was something Wenzel would have to repeat time and again as the beer grew more popular. "There's a reason they call it craft beer," he said. In keeping with the handcraft, Lion's Tail introduced the concept of bar top dry hopping in 2016. Customers select their hop of choice and, using a French press, perform their own dry hopping with a pint of the brewery's Custom Pale Ale.

By 2017, Wenzel had become enamored with a new style of beer yet to have been produced by a local brewery. He had been introduced to New England–style IPAs by Eric Henzel, Wenzel's brother-in-law and the brewery's general manager. The highly aromatic, hop-infused style proceeds from a complex interplay of water chemistry, yeast and hops. It was the sort of deep-dive the former chemical engineer was looking for. Released in the Lion's Tail taproom in September 2017, Juice Cloud was the first New England–style IPA brewed commercially in Winnebago County. The beer immediately became the brewery's best seller and garnered a couple of regional awards. "I've been evolving that recipe," Wenzel said. "It lets me apply some of the principles of science that give me kind of a different edge than other brewers. It's going to be fun to keep playing with."

The adventurous spirit Wenzel brought from homebrewing inspires how he runs his brewery. "I know we have to be smart about the business aspect," he said. "I have our life savings invested in this. But at the same time, I've seen it happen where people get too caught up in making money and become slaves to the business end of it. That's when you lose what made you unique in the first place. That's my biggest fear; to get stale, and to lose the love of brewing and treat it just as a business. I'm not going to let that happen."

FIFTH WARD BREWING COMPANY

1009 South Main Street, Oshkosh

In 2013, a couple of young homebrewers showed up at the August meeting of the Society of Oshkosh Brewers. Ian Wenger and Zach Clark were both twenty-two. They had started homebrewing about a year earlier. They already had big plans, saying they were going to open a brewery. That kind of talk is often floated at homebrew club meetings. Most often it drifts away. Not this time.

"Before we even brewed our first batch, we were looking into what it would take to open a brewery," Wenger said. "We were doing things like pricing out kegs and emailing farmers about where we were going to dump our massive amounts of spent grains. Big dreams." Realizing the dream would take time, which they had, and money, which they didn't. Clark and Wenger were students at the University of Wisconsin–Oshkosh and used the university's small business development center to get help with their business plan and make connections with potential investors. They were laying a foundation piece by piece.

By 2015, Clark and Wenger's plan had progressed well beyond pipe-dream status. They were scouting properties and meeting with professional brewers to learn all they could. Russ Klisch, president of Milwaukee's Lakefront Brewery, became a mentor. "We've been doing our homework figuring out costs and poking into every little corner of what we need to do to get this up and running," Wenger said at the time. "We have a very clear idea of what we want this to be, our brand, and the types of beer we'll sell."

Clark and Wenger began getting the word out on what they were up to. They visited local taverns, gifting bar managers bottles of their homebrew as a way of introduction. Within a couple months, they collected eight letters of intent from taverns interested in purchasing their beer. They took their beer on the homebrew festival circuit, seeking the unvarnished opinions of strangers. "That was something we really came to enjoy," Clark said. "It was great to be able to get that kind of immediate feedback on the recipes we were developing."

At those festivals, they'd tack a Fifth Ward Brewing Company banner to the front of their table. Clark and Wenger had come up with the name early on. The home they were renting was located just a couple blocks away from where Christian Kaehler had built his Fifth Ward Brewery in 1858. "It's where we learned how to brew," Clark said. "The name is an ode to that and a nod to the history of brewing in Oshkosh. We want to keep that alive."

By the spring of 2016, most of the pieces were in place. Clark and Wenger had teamed with Maurice Berglund, who became their primary investor and cofounder. Over the previous year, Berglund had gotten to know and homebrew with Clark and Wenger. "Observing their work ethic and seeing their passion, I kind of fell in love with them, so to speak," Berglund said.

"Next thing you know, we were working on business plans." They selected a South Main Street location for the brewery. The building they moved into and began renovating was in a decaying industrial sector that was about to get a major overhaul. Fifth Ward Brewing would be a linchpin in the redevelopment.

On October 20, 2017, Clark and Wenger brewed their first batch on their new, oversized ten-barrel system. The beer was Hades' Secret, a porter brewed with additions of chocolate and mint. It was one of the homebrew

Right: Zach Clark *(left)* and Ian Wenger getting the Fifth Ward brewhouse ready in advance of the brewery's opening.

Below: Zach Clark *(left)* and Ian Wenger on November 9, 2017, opening day at Fifth Ward Brewing.

recipes they'd developed while working in the kitchen at Dublin's Irish Pub in Oshkosh. Fifth Ward's early beers were heavily influenced by Clark and Wenger's cooking background and often featured culinary techniques and ingredients. The lineup included a brown ale made with molasses and cinnamon and a wheat ale brewed with honey and spiced with saffron.

The Fifth Ward taproom opened to the public on November 9, 2017. The influx of patrons over the coming months exceeded expectations. Meanwhile, the early legwork was paying dividends. Fifth Ward beers began popping up on tap in Winnebago County taverns. Those young brewers used to show up at the bar with bottles of their homebrew in tow. Now they came wheeling in kegs of fresh beer straight from their brewery. It's not all that different from the way Horn and Schwalm had done things on the south side of Oshkosh 150 years earlier. Clark and Wenger took up that legacy and made it their own.

OMEGA BREWING EXPERIENCE

115 East Main Street, Omro

The Editor of [the *Omro Union*] *has been, ever since we knew him, howling, in his feeble way, over the sale of liquor in that place, and damning every man who had anything to do with the unclean thing.*
—Eureka Journal, *April 29, 1868*

That's just the way it was in Omro. No other town in Winnebago County ever harbored such a severe antiliquor streak as that village on the Fox River did in the latter half of the nineteenth century. Omro's saloon keepers, beer bottlers and liquor dealers were constantly harassed and sometimes outlawed by the powers that be. No one dared put a brewery there. Then Steve Zink came along.

In 2015, Zink was a homebrewer seriously thinking about ratcheting up his hobby into something more extreme. He had people urging him on, including his son Eric, whom he sometimes brewed with. "We came out of the chute with some pretty good beers," Zink said. Then he laughs. "We made some pretty bad ones, too, but that's all part of learning. Anyway, I started getting a lot of positive feedback, and I thought when I retire I might as well look at starting up a brewery and seeing what we could do."

Zink didn't wait for retirement. An engineer by trade, he began dedicating his time away from work into what he hoped would become his post-retirement career. He registered the name Omega Brewing Experience in 2015 and began hunting for a location. When he found an old meat market sitting vacant on Main Street in Omro, he decided to go for it. By the time Zink had purchased the property in the spring of 2016, he had already met with the Omro Planning Commission to discuss his idea for bringing a brewery to the village. Times had changed. Zink was welcomed with open arms.

The next couple of years were spent renovating the interior of the ninety-year-old building. Much of the work was done by Zink and his wife, Kathy. His job kept him on the road most weekdays, so weekends turned into bouts of labor dedicated to what had become a second job. "Anything that you see here was not here when we bought the building," Zink said, standing in his brewery. "Every wall has been taken down, and the floors taken up. We cleared this place out and entirely redesigned it." Thankfully, it wasn't too large of a space, but that was intentional. "I wanted to focus on the brewing process instead of getting a massive building," Zink said.

Steve Zink in the taproom–brew house of Omega Brewing Experience.

By January 2018, it was beginning to feel like a brewery. Zink was working on a one-barrel system, a comfortable step up from his homebrewing setup. "It's like a higher scale homebrew process," Zink said. The first beers began pouring in Oshkosh at Pilora's Café, where Cory Tellock, Zink's son-in-law and sometimes brewing partner, works as a chef. Zink went into an intense period of brewing, building up a catalog of beers for the anticipated opening of his taproom that shares space with the brewery. The beers reflected Zink's expansive tastes. "I like 'em all," he said. "We'll cover the spectrum from American cream ale, to Belgian dubbels, and imperial stouts. We'll even eventually get into some barrel aging."

On April 7, 2018, Omega Brewing Experience opened the doors to its taproom. Zink made no formal announcement of the opening, he simply flipped the sign hanging in the window that had read "Closed" for the past two years. He had eight of his brews ready to pour. A few of them, like his double IPA and his French saison, represented styles that hadn't been served on draft in Omro before. At first, people trickled in, but as word spread, they began coming in droves. By the close of the following day, they had consumed nearly everything Zink had brewed. Omro finally had its brewery. Too bad the old editor of the *Omro Union* couldn't have been there to add his howling to the excitement.

HighHolder Brewing

2211 Oregon Street, Oshkosh

The new breweries have fostered a sense of community around them that was lost long before the brewery failures of the 1970s. But with HighHolder Brewing, the connection to place is even more fundamental. HighHolder is an expression of the beer culture it grew out of. If you were into good beer and lived on the south side of Oshkosh in the early 2000s, chances are you were acquainted with Mike Schlosser and Shawn O'Marro. They were fixtures on the south-side Oshkosh beer scene years before their brewery came into being.

O'Marro had opened O'Marro's Public House in 2004. It was the first tavern on the south side to feature craft beer. "Back then, you could hardly get people to drink anything that was even slightly dark," Brandy O'Marro, Shawn's wife, recalls. "I think we were the only bar in Oshkosh that didn't have Miller Lite on tap. We were told we'd never make it. Not in this town." The O'Marros did just fine. Their pub turned into a hangout for beer geeks and homebrewers. Mike Schlosser was both. Schlosser had already been homebrewing for a dozen years and was a member of the Society of Oshkosh Brewers, which held its club meetings at O'Marro's Public House. As O'Marro and Schlosser got to know one another, they began kicking around the idea of starting a brewery based in O'Marro's pub. "It just seemed like the obvious thing for us to do at some point," Shawn O'Marro said. "A brewery was the next logical step for us to take."

It would be a while before they hit their stride. "We had a good idea of what we wanted to do, but we were just totally naive about how to get it done," Schlosser said. What O'Marro and Schlosser wanted to do was practically unheard of. In 2006, there existed a rigid set of norms for starting a brewery. It entailed the acquisition of a ten- to thirty-barrel brewing system, packaging equipment, a distribution agreement and a mountain of debt. That was not what O'Marro and Schlosser had in mind. "We didn't want to end up living in a cardboard box to do this," Schlosser said. What they wanted was to establish a nano-brewery, a term yet to enter the brewing lexicon when O'Marro and Schlosser began talking about it. They were going to brew

Shawn O'Marro *(left)* and Mike Schlosser in 2015 in front of the brew system Schlosser was building for HighHolder brewing.

Mike Schlosser *(left)* and Shawn O'Marro in their brewhouse at HighHolder.

beer on a small system that could produce a barrel or less, package it in kegs and sell it on draft in O'Marro's pub. By 2015, the idea of nano-brewing had become widely accepted, and O'Marro and Schlosser were on track to open the first such brewery in Winnebago County. But a good part of the next three years was spent trying to navigate a legal quagmire created by a 2011 change to Wisconsin law that impeded a tavern owner's involvement with a brewery. O'Marro's ownership of the pub presented difficulties. They hired lawyers. That didn't help. "We took our lumps," Schlosser said. "It took us six months just to clean up the mess the lawyers made."

On February 8, 2018, they finally made it through with the last of their required permits being issued. HighHolder Brewing opened for business in a suite connected to O'Marro's Public House. "I've been fighting this for so long I kind of have the 'wait what?' feeling," Schlosser said at the time.

The new brewery's name was an homage to the south side of Oshkosh. The original high holders were beer-loving Bavarian and Bohemian immigrants who settled on Oshkosh's south side in the late 1800s. They congregated in an area that came to be known as the Bloody Sixth Ward. When the brewery made its official debut on tap at O'Marro's Public House on March 16, 2018, the beer they poured was HighHolder's Bloody Sixth Irish Red Ale.

Like the first breweries established in Winnebago County, HighHolder Brewing emerged from within a community closely identified with beer. But as those early breweries grew larger, their links to their communities withered. In 1972, after all of the breweries were gone, the county's beer culture looked to have run its course. Not so—the restoration of that culture may have been unforeseen, but drinking HighHolder beer at O'Marro's pub makes the revival seem as if it were inevitable.

ONWARD

At the time of this writing at the end of spring in 2018, there are six breweries operating in Winnebago County. There haven't been that many breweries in the county since 1894. But that time bears little resemblance to the contemporary period. The 1890s were a time of intense consolidation. The breweries were growing larger and becoming dependent upon distribution beyond their home base. Smaller, community-focused breweries were being forced out. At the same time, brewers and the drinking public were becoming increasingly conservative in their tastes. Pale lagers were coming to the fore and would override all other styles of beer.

None of this is congruent with our current time. A more appropriate benchmark may be the 1870s, when more than a dozen breweries in Winnebago County produced a broad range of beers from dark lagers to pale, sour ales. Today, it's a given that each brewery will make an even wider range of beers. And like the earlier period, these beers are being served to customers at the brewery where they are made.

Perhaps the most explicit connection to the past is the way in which the contemporary breweries connect with the people living around them. Those relationships are as direct as they were in 1857, when Fischer and Kaehler invited their neighbors to visit their brewery to taste the bock beer they had just made. This kind of thing is again a regular event.

Since 1849, Winnebago County has been home to thirty-one breweries. The tradition of local beer has proven incredibly durable. Today, that tradition remains as vibrant as ever. Prost!

SELECTED BIBLIOGRAPHY

Adams, Arva Luther, Caryl Chandler Herziger and Winifred Anderson Pawloski, eds. *A Tale of Twin Cities: The Development of the Fox River Waterway.* Neenah, WI: Neenah Historical Society, 1993.

Akin, Ron, and Lee Reiherzer. *The Breweries of Oshkosh, Their Rise and Fall.* Oshkosh, WI: Akin/Reiherzer, 2012.

Apps, Jerry. *Breweries of Wisconsin.* Madison: University of Wisconsin Press, 1992.

Auer, James M. *Centennial Memories: A Brief History of Menasha, Wisconsin.* Menasha, WI: Auer, 1953.

Baron, Stanley Wade. *Brewed in America: A History of Beer and Ale in the United States.* Boston: Little, Brown, 1962.

Christianson, Peter L., and Karen C. Christianson, eds. *History of the Town of Winchester, Winnebago County, Wisconsin.* Larson, WI: Winchester Area Historical Society, 2002.

Cochran, Thomas C. *The Pabst Brewing Company: The History of an American Business.* New York: New York University Press, 1948.

Cole, Harry E. *Stagecoach and Tavern Tales of the Old Northwest.* Carbondale: Southern Illinois University Press, 1930.

Coughlin, James P. *Triumphs and Tragedies in the History of Winneconne, 1848–1983.* Winneconne, WI: Coughlin, 1983.

Cross, Scott. *Like a Deer Chased by Dogs: The Life of Chief Oshkosh.* Oshkosh, WI: Oshkosh Public Museum, 2002.

Cunningham, Gustavus A. *History of Neenah, Illustrated.* Neenah, WI: Gazette Printing Establishment, 1878.

Decker, Henry Jr., and George B. Goodwin, eds. *The Village of Menasha, Its Location, History, and Advantages*. Menasha, WI: D.C. Felton, 1857.

Draeger, Jim, and Mark Speltz. *Bottoms Up: A Toast to Wisconsin's Historic Bars and Breweries*. Madison: Wisconsin Historical Society, 2012.

Goc, Michael J. *In This Century: A History of Winnebago County in the 20th Century*. Friendship, WI: New Past Press, 1998.

———. *Land Rich Enough: An Illustrated History of Oshkosh and Winnebago County*. Chatsworth, CA: Windsor Publications, 1988.

———. *Oshkosh at 150: An Illustrated History of Oshkosh*. Friendship, WI: New Past Press, 2003.

Harney, Richard J. *History of Winnebago County, Wisconsin, and Early History of the Northwest*. Oshkosh, WI: Allen & Hicks, 1880.

Hieronymus, Stan. *For the Love of Hops: The Practical Guide to Aroma, Bitterness and the Culture of Hops*. Boulder: Brewers Publications, 2012.

History of the Town of Clayton, Winnebago County, Wisconsin. Larson, WI: Winchester Area Historical Society, 1999.

Kay, Bob, Tye Schwalbe, John Steiner and Herb Page. *Wisconsin Beer Labels, the First 75 Years*. Batavia, IL: Bob Kay Beer Labels, 2013.

Kroll, Wayne L. *Badger Breweries Past and Present*. Jefferson, WI: Kroll, 1976.

———. *Wisconsin's Frontier Farm Breweries, 1830's–1880's*. Fort Atkinson, WI: Kroll, 2003.

Lawson, Publius V. *History, Winnebago County, Wisconsin: Its Cities, Towns, Resources, People*. Chicago: C.F. Cooper, 1908.

Mallett, John. *Malt: A Practical Guide from Field to Brewhouse*. Boulder: Brewers Publications, 2014.

McKay, Tom, and Deborah E. Kmetz, eds. *Agricultural Diversity in Wisconsin*. Madison: State Historical Society of Wisconsin, 1987.

Metz, James I. *Oshkosh Aflame! Traumas and Triumphs of Its Sawdust Citizens*. Oshkosh, WI: Polemics Press, 1999.

———, ed. *Prairie, Pines, and People: Winnebago County in a New Perspective*. Oshkosh, WI: Oshkosh Northwestern, 1976.

Mittelman, Amy. *Brewing Battles: A History of American Beer*. New York: Algora Publishing, 2008.

Ogle, Maureen. *Ambitious Brew: The Story of American Beer*. Orlando: Houghton Mifflin Harcourt, 2006.

One Hundred Years of Brewing. Chicago: H.S. Rich, 1901.

Pattinson, Ronald. *Decoction!* Amsterdam: Kilderkin, 2012.

Powers, Madelon. *Faces along the Bar: Lore and Order in the Workingman's Saloon, 1870–1920*. Chicago: University of Chicago Press, 1998.

Rogers, Daisy. *Index to Winneconne, 1849–1949*. Winneconne, WI: K. Grace, 2002.

Shattuck, S.F., ed. *A History of Neenah*. Neenah, WI: Neenah Historical Society, 1958.

Spanbauer, Larry. *Oshkosh Neighborhood Taverns and the People Who Ran Them*. Oshkosh, WI: Spanbauer, 2012.

Tomlan, Michael A. *Tinged with Gold: Hop Culture in the United States*. Athens: University of Georgia Press, 1992.

Tremblay, Victor J., and Carol Horton Tremblay. *The US Brewing Industry Data and Economic Analysis*. Cambridge, MA: The MIT Press, 2009.

Van Wieren, Dale P., ed. *American Breweries II*. West Point, PA.: Eastern Coast Breweriana Association, 1995.

Wahl, Arnold Spencer, and Robert Wahl. *Beer from the Expert's Viewpoint*. Chicago: Wahl Institute, 1937.

Wahl, Robert, and Max Henius. *American Handy-Book of the Brewing, Malting and Auxiliary Trades*. Chicago: Wahl & Henius, 1902.

Zeitlin, Richard H. *Germans in Wisconsin*. Madison: State Historical Society of Wisconsin, 1977.

INDEX

ABOUT THE AUTHOR

Lee Reiherzer's fondness for all things beer developed after his father gave him a taste of Bohemian Club Lager. That sip triggered a lifelong interest in beer and brewing history. He began writing about beer in 2010 after launching the Oshkosh Beer website and has since written dozens of articles about his favorite subject for numerous print and online publications. In 2012, he coauthored the book *The Breweries of Oshkosh, Their Rise and Fall.* In his spare time, Reiherzer enjoys hop cultivation and is an award-winning homebrewer who loves brewing the old-time lagers that were once revered in Winnebago County. He and his wife, Denise Lanthier, make their home in Oshkosh.